Routedge Revivals

The Truth about China and Japan

This title, first published in 1921, aimed to present for the reader a glance into what the position was in Eastern Asia at the beginning of the twentieth century. This book will be of interest to student of history, politics and Asian Studies.

The Truth about China and Japan

Putnam Weale

First published in 1921
by George Allen & Unwin

This edition first published in 2015 by Routledge
2 Park Square, Milton Park, Abingdon, Oxon, OX14 4RN
and by Routledge
711 Third Avenue, New York, NY 10017

Routledge is an imprint of the Taylor & Francis Group, an informa business

© 1921 Putnam Weale

All rights reserved. No part of this book may be reprinted or reproduced or utilised in any form or by any electronic, mechanical, or other means, now known or hereafter invented, including photocopying and recording, or in any information storage or retrieval system, without permission in writing from the publishers.

Publisher's Note
The publisher has gone to great lengths to ensure the quality of this reprint but points out that some imperfections in the original copies may be apparent.

Disclaimer
The publisher has made every effort to trace copyright holders and welcomes correspondence from those they have been unable to contact.

A Library of Congress record exists under LC control number: 19015104

ISBN 13: 978-1-138-91250-2 (hbk)
ISBN 13: 978-1-315-69187-9 (ebk)
ISBN 13: 978-1-138-91252-6 (pbk)

THE TRUTH ABOUT CHINA AND JAPAN

BY
PUTNAM WEALE

LONDON: GEORGE ALLEN & UNWIN LTD.
RUSKIN HOUSE, 40 MUSEUM STREET, W.C.1

COPYRIGHT, 1919, NEW YORK
BY DODD, MEAD AND COMPANY, INC.

First published in Great Britain . . . 1921

All rights reserved)

PREFACE

THE present volume has been written primarily to allow the ordinary reader to see at a glance what the position really is to-day in Eastern Asia, and to explain precisely why there should be conflict between China and Japan.

The essential point—which the writer first insisted upon at great length in *The Fight for the Republic in China*—is that Japan has a dual policy, one policy for the East and another for the West; that she uses military power and secret loans to advance the first, and diplomacy and publicity the second; and that this intricate matter can be understood only by exploring the history of the remote past and linking it up with what is taking place to-day. The fact that the Imperial Conference, which has just concluded its labours, failed to reach any unanimous conclusions on the subject of Japan gives additional point to the arguments which follow, and demands that the important group of documents in the Appendix—particularly the Anglo-Japanese Treaty —be studied in the light of this new development.

LONDON,
September, 1921.

CONTENTS

CHAPTER	PAGE
I. GENERAL INTRODUCTION: THE EARLY RELATIONS BETWEEN CHINA AND JAPAN	9
II. THE OUTLINE OF THE FAR EAST	47
III. THE SETTLEMENT OF THE CHINESE QUESTION	68
IV. THE PROBLEM OF PEKING	85
V. IF JAPAN REFUSES?	105

APPENDIX:
- A. The Anglo-Japanese Alliance Treaty, 125.
- B. Text of the Lansing-Ishii Notes, 127.
- C. Japanese Secret Loans to China in 1918, 129.
- D. The Shantung Railway Agreement of September 24, 1918, 132.
- E. Kirin and Heilungchiang Mining and Forestry Agreement, 135.
- F. Articles from the Japanese Constitution Defining the Autocracy of the Japanese Government, 137.
- G. The Manchurian and Mongolian (Secret) Railway Agreement, 139.
- H. The Shantung Railway Extension Agreement, 143.
- I. Text of Sino-Japanese Wireless Installation Agreement, 147.

The Truth about China and Japan

CHAPTER I

GENERAL INTRODUCTION—EARLY RELATIONS OF CHINESE AND JAPANESE

THE best authorities are agreed that the ancient Chinese originally migrated from a point near the Caspian Sea across what is now arid desert to the upper reaches of the Yellow River. The date at which this exodus took place is so remote that all trace of it has been lost; and although the proofs of the Central Asian origin of the race are satisfying to scholars, they are of a nature which cannot be here adequately summarized. Excavations recently made in Honan province have, however, brought to light utensils and modellings in baked clay of the most primitive description, including Noah's arks of almost Biblical exactitude. According to some experts, these are conclusive evidence not only of a settlement which may be counted at least six thousand years old, but point to a close cultural connection with very distant regions. It may be that systematic search will some day disclose new and remarkable facts concerning Chinese origins in the cradle of the human race.

In any case it is quite certain that thirty centuries before the Christian era the Chinese had already occupied most of the territory comprised in the modern provinces of Kansu, Shensi, and Honan; that their route eastwards—towards the sea—was barred by forests may be assumed. It is interesting to record that their pictorial character for " East " is a sun shining through trees, whilst the word " obstruction " is compounded by placing the selfsame tree in a doorway. The remote ancestors of the race certainly cleared the land as they advanced, changing from a pastoral cultivator race, tilling the soil in small patches, into a purely agricultural nation at a time when classical Greece had not yet emerged out of the dim mists. The Chinese still venerate the name of the ruler who established tillage as the basic institution, and who rightly assumed that there is no increment so rich and so beneficial to mankind as the increment of the fields.

Twenty-five hundred years ago, when Confucius and Laotzu flourished, China was already a very old country. Although the celebrated Stone Drums in the Confucian Temple in Peking, which are said to record the hunting adventures of an emperor of the Chou dynasty (876 B.C.), show the most ancient writing known, it is probable that the transition from tying knots on cords, as a means of conveying ideas, to cutting notches on wood, and finally to writing pictorial and ideographic symbols, took place many centuries earlier. The conception of a central kingship was certainly well fixed by the time of the first emperors of the Hsia dynasty (2200 B.C.); and Confucius, writing in the sixth century before Christ on the discontents of the age,

GENERAL INTRODUCTION 11

constantly bewails the spacious days of the legendary rulers Yao and Shun, who ruled as shepherd kings anterior to the Hsia. Remembering how much older the human race is to-day admitted to be than was believed a generation ago, it is by no means improbable that the Chinese entered the Yellow River valley at least a hundred centuries ago.

This ancient people of the pre-Christian era was a small, warring community of not more than a few million souls. Distributed along the loess soil of the broad, central valleys, their expansion during a very long period was hardly noticeable, wars and expeditions tending to monopolize their attention and breaking up the country into petty states in spite of the Imperial rule. The North China of to-day was then nothing but an arid frontierland, a glacis; and the present metropolitan province of Chihli as wild as much of Mongolia still is. That barbarian raiders from the wastes of Central Asia were aspest from the earliest times, and harried the race as soon as it had acquired ease and wealth from tillage, may be gathered from the policy of the Emperor Chin Shih Huang-ti (249–206 B.C.). It was this ruler who is still celebrated in the Annals for two dissimilar yet closely-related acts: he burned China's classics, because they were bringing decadence to the race, and began the building of the Great Wall as a protection for his newly formed Empire.

The oldest capitals of China, Hsianfu in Shensi and Loyang in Honan, were soon directly protected by this vast rampart, which was methodically extended by succeeding dynasties, until in the time of the Mings the last gap between the Mongolian mountains and the sea was finally closed at Shanhaikwan. Yet neither the Great Wall nor the great sacrifice of learning was of much avail: the Chinese were to be a constant prey to more warlike peoples. The quietist characteristics of the race had indeed become unalterably fixed in the long-ago, their own wars and disputes tending to have a municipal rather than a national character.

China's nearest neighbour in these early times was Korea, lying to the north-east; and a vast amount of Far Eastern history pivots on this fact. Whilst it is true that Chinese adventurers, sailing down from the Yangtsze estuary, began to get into touch with the Annamese and aboriginal kingdoms around Canton soon after the Christian era, the land routes southwards were still barred by mountainous country, filled with fierce peoples. The Koreans were more docile. Broken up into small communities living in caves, culture was brought to them by Chinese scholars two thousand years ago; and their genius was sufficiently literary to allow them almost immediately to evolve an alphabet of their own for their polysyllabic dialect. That they flourished and grew in numbers rapidly is proved by the fact that they had colonized all the region of Southern Manchuria called the Liaotung fifteen hundred years ago, advancing to within a few miles of Shanhaikwan. Always famous as miners, their workings can still be seen in extra-mural Chihli; and so well known was their quest for the precious metals that Kheraded-Bey, an Arabian traveller of the eighth century, described Silla (Korea) as being rich in gold.

It was the first of the four Manchurian-Mongolian races, who successfully conquered North China and

GENERAL INTRODUCTION 13

established dynasties, who broke Korea's land-contact with the Chinese. The Kitan Tartars in the year 1012 took the Liaotung peninsula and all the territory west of the Yalu River, driving the Koreans back into their original abode. The present boundaries of Korea were therefore fixed more than nine hundred years ago. The Kitans, who soon penetrated into North China, handed on their sovereignty to another Tartar tribe, the Chin Tartars, who were just as short-lived, but established themselves firmly north of the Yellow River. Then came the Mongol or Yuan dynasty; and when this dynasty was finally expelled by the Mings in the fourteenth century, the Chinese colonization of Manchuria was greatly developed, with the transference of the national capital from Nanking back to Peking (1412). Just as Chihli and the Mongolian border-lands had been settled in previous centuries, so now did the plains of the Tartars receive in large numbers the Sons of Han.

This Manchurian colonization was, however, limited to the Liaotung, i.e. the country east of the Liao River, and to the districts immediately adjoining it. Beyond—in the mountains and forests—lurked fierce tribes ever ready to raid their peaceful neighbours. The Chinese symbols of conquest were now as in the dim past the mattock and the plough; their permanent posture was one of defence carried on from inside walled cities. In the sixteenth century began their historic struggle with the Manchus, a race of mountaineers living at the foot of the Ever White mountain, who finally repeated the miracle of Kublai Khan and his Tartars and conquered the Empire after a conflict lasting two generations.

The first census taken by the Manchus in 1651,

14 THE TRUTH ABOUT CHINA AND JAPAN

after the restoration of order, returned China's population at 55 million persons, which is less than the number given in the first census of the Han dynasty, A.D. 1, and about the same as when Kublai Khan established the Mongol dynasty in 1295. Thus we are faced by the amazing fact that, from the beginning of the Christian era, the toll of life taken by internecine and frontier wars in China was so great that in spite of all territorial expansion the population for upwards of sixteen centuries remained more or less stationary. There is in all history no similar record. Now, however, came a vast change. Thus three years after the death of the celebrated Manchu emperor Kang Hsi, in 1720, the population had risen to 125 millions. At the beginning of the reign of the no less illustrious Ch'ien Lung (1743) it was returned at 145 millions; towards the end of his reign in 1783 it had doubled, and was given as 283 millions. In the reign of Chia Ch'ing (1812) it had risen to 360 millions; before the Taiping Rebellion (1842) it had grown to 413 millions; after that terrible rising it sunk to 261 millions. Thus good government between the years 1651 and 1842—a period of 191 years—increased China's population from 55 millions to 413 millions, an eightfold growth. It had been left to a foreign race to achieve this surprising result.

II

Who are the Japanese? For political reasons the Japanese trace their emperors from a sun-goddess who is supposed to have come from Korea in the seventh century B.C. There is a great deal more in myths than is generally supposed, and there is no reason to doubt that the earliest connection between the Asiatic mainland and Southern Japan was expressed in the terms of an armed invasion led by a queen. In any case it is generally accepted that the Japanese are partly descended from a double stream of immigrants who came from the mainland by way of Korea, one stream being Manchu-Korean and the other Mongol; but Baelz, one of the most distinguished investigators of Japanese origins, finds from the recording of many cephalic indices and from other biometrical data that the strongest strain in the people is undoubtedly Malay.

If you strip off the outer Chinese clothing of both men and women (the kimono is a direct importation from China made during the Tang dynasty) you make a remarkable discovery. The men wear a loin-cloth peculiar to all the water-peoples of the island-groups along the shores of Southern Asia; whilst the women have on what is nothing more or less than the Malay *sarong*, or skirts, and a little sleeveless jacket. Garbed like this, and placed on the curved Malay fishing-boats still in use, you see the original invaders as they floated up from their southern islands on the *Kuroshiwo*, or black current which washes their shores. In their houses, raised two feet above the ground, you may trace the vestigial remains of the water-house built on piles; and although the Japanese share with the Koreans the habit of removing their shoes indoors and sitting on matted floors, their peculiar wooden clogs, with the separated big toe, are plainly the invention of a barefooted people treading the forest trails, and needing at a moment's notice to be able to free their feet for tree-climbing.

It is necessary to dwell on these details in order to fix well the differences between the Chinese and the Japanese. The Chinese almost from the dawn of history are a race of peaceful cultivators, walling themselves in for defence; the Japanese are a water-people, who become a forest-folk and who hunt and fish and only learn agriculture reluctantly. At the beginning of the Christian era, thinly scattered in the valleys and along the coasts of their own islands, they had not yet driven out the aborigines we know as the Ainus, and warfare against them was constant and intense. Being rude and unlettered, there are few traces of their early history. But from this dim forest past comes the Japanese *torii*, that curious structure originally made of tree-trunks—which so many mistake for a gateway—which was erected in front of the sun-goddess's shrines so that fowls might perch on it and salute at dawn the first rays of the rising sun.

Chinese history shows that between the years 57 and 247 of our era Japan sent four embassies to the Courts of the Han and Wei dynasties; but it is not until the sixth century that the light on the relations between Japan and China begins to grow clear. With the spread of Buddhism from across the Yellow Sea came the first real knowledge of the Chinese classics, the Japanese written language by means of Chinese ideographs dating only from the seventh century. Prior to that there are certain evidences that the peculiar Korean script was fitfully borrowed, although it never really took root.

It is learning, then, that forms the first bridge between China and Japan, and in this learning Buddhism plays a great and important part. Priests and scholars crossed in great numbers from China, giving religion, which had been hitherto expressed in the crude Shinto forest-rites, a new and more imposing significance. There was a constant stream of immigrants crossing by way of Korea; Chinese temples begin to be built; and the result of this cultural intercourse may be gathered from the fact that a census of the Japanese nobility, taken in A.D. 814, indicated 382 Korean and Chinese families against 796 of purely Japanese origin. The governmental institutions of China were likewise borrowed, the eight departments of state being copied from the T'ang dynasty in China, which is famous in Japanese annals for its civilizing influence. At the beginning of the eighth century the first Japanese capital was built at Nara on the accepted Chinese plan of a metropolis, with nine gates and nine avenues, the palace being placed in the northern section and approached by a broad straight avenue dividing the city into two perfectly equal parts. During the ensuing centuries Japan was completely transformed by the adoption of Chinese civilization, foppishness in dress and a great growth of luxury distinguishing the period. That Chinese suzerainty was admitted is not disputed, China enjoying under the T'ang a greater cultural supremacy in Eastern Asia than ever before or since.

So it lasted for more than three hundred years. Then a great change took place in the character of Japan owing to the feudal era, which was brought about by the struggle for power between leading families and by the intensified warfare with the Ainu barbarians. A certain Yorimoto in the twelfth century first obtained the title of *Sei-itai-shogun* (Barbarian-subduing Generalissimo), and just as the office of Regent had long been hereditary in the Fujiwara family, who gave the emperors their empresses by prescriptive right, so now did the office of Shogun belong to the Minamoto family, who established a capital at Kamakura.

The result of these facts—that militarism so early acquired a special character having all the strength of an established ritual—tinges all Japanese history, and begins that long dualism in government which still lives on under the present modern Constitution. After a period of Chinese culture, the first characteristics of the race reassert themselves, and the history of the strongest clans becomes the history of Japan. The Court, sinking as Chinese Courts were wont to sink into a purely ceremonial office, is pushed more and more into the background; and rival Shoguns, taking the field against one another and acquiring ever greater strength through the growth of the hereditary warrior-class, split up the country into great fiefs.

Relations with China, which had been cordial and intimate during the formative period, now greatly diminished in cordiality. We know that during the Yuan or Mongol dynasty two expeditions, which failed disastrously, were sent to Japan in order to enforce the claims of suzerainty. This left behind a heritage of hatred which never disappeared. True, under the Ashikaga Shoguns, in the fourteenth, fifteenth, and sixteenth centuries,

GENERAL INTRODUCTION

increasing importance was attached to trade with China so as to defray the costs of the interminable civil wars. The Ming dynasty, when its capital was at Nanking, was induced, although Japanese piracy was constant, to grant commercial passports to facilitate this intercourse, Japanese swordblades significantly forming the principal article in the Japanese export trade. It was at the end of the fourteenth century, when relations had been reopened, after a formal protest by China at the continued piracy practised, that there occurred that remarkable event, the investiture of the Shogun Yoshimitsu by a Chinese envoy with a royal diploma and a crown. No event in Japanese history has attracted more attention than this. That the Shogun, who in point of dynastic law was simply the emperor's " protector," performed this act mainly to consolidate his own usurpation seems to-day clear; but the minute and careful regulations which the Ming emperors issued regarding the tribute vessels from Japan—to prevent armed conspiracies—prove that on the Chinese side there was no doubt about Japanese vassalage. Certain it is that, as the years passed, relations between China and Japan steadily diminished in cordiality, and contact became more and more distant, save in the singular and supremely important matter of Korea.

III

A glance at the map will show how inevitable it has been that Korea should have played so large a part in the political history of the Far East. The peninsula, which juts out in such an astonishing way, somewhat after the fashion of Italy in Europe, is separated from Japan by only 120 miles of water. If, however, the island of Tsushima, which divides the straits into two channels, is included, as well as smaller islands such as Iki, it may be said that when passing between the two countries land is hardly ever out of sight. This is an important consideration: in olden times it had political consequences of the most far-reaching nature.

The Chinese claims of suzerainty in Korea had never been disputed. In primitive days, for instance during the T'ang dynasty, the expression of China's suzerain rights may only have had a fugitive character: yet it was none the less undeniable. The ancient method of a small country admitting suzerainty was simply the dispatch of periodic embassies carrying tribute or gifts, and by this ceremonious act acquiring the right of protection against alien aggression. Korea had sent such missions to her great neighbour, who had given her civilization, from the time of the Han dynasty: and during the wars between the several Korean kingdoms in the sixth century, Chinese troops had not only participated in the struggle but had driven out the Southern dynasty, which was supported by Japanese warriors, making all Korea nominally a Chinese province.

The period of Tartar domination in North China, first under the Kitan, then under the Chin Tartars, broke up the traditional relationship between China and Korea. But no sooner was the Mongol dynasty well established than it revived the old customs, and received homage, Korea aiding and abetting the expeditions against Japan.

Under the Ming dynasty the intimate ceremonious relations between China and Korea were re-established on a firmer basis than ever before; for in 1392 a new Korean dynasty had arisen, and the first emperor tendered his homage and accepted the Chinese calendar and chronology as a sign of his submission. From then on investiture of the Korean sovereigns was regular and formal, no succession being legitimate until it had Chinese Imperial sanction. Korea became so thoroughly saturated with Chinese culture that the Korean dress of to-day is still based on Ming models, the old Chinese topknot being left on Korean heads when the Manchus conquered Korea in 1637 (before they had entered China) as an act of grace because the Koreans had submitted so promptly.

The great and growing friction between China and Japan which was evident during the Ming period, and which was signalized by Japanese raiders in 1554 landing on the Kiangsu and Chekiang coasts south of the Yangtsze and capturing a number of towns, brought the inevitable result in Korea. Japanese raiding in the peninsula during the sixteenth century became more and more frequent, finally culminating in the great and hideous Hideyoshi expedition, which is such an outstanding feature in Far Eastern relations that it must be dealt with at some length.

The great commander Hideyoshi, taking advantage of the feudal militarism, had subdued all Japan, and by 1592 had massed an immense army of 300,000 which he was determined to use abroad.

His original design was undoubtedly not the conquest of Korea but the conquest of China. Korea was simply the stepping-stone, and had Korea consented to be put to such a use she need never have suffered as she did. The Koreans of the sixteenth century were, however, loyal to their Chinese commitments, and just as Belgium of the twentieth century refused to be made a passage-way for the German armies into France, so did Korea refuse to allow Hideyoshi a free hand, and desperately resisted. Her castles and her armies were destroyed one after another, the Japanese advance finally reaching Pingyang, although never going beyond.

It was Korean sea-power which finally saved the nation. The Chinese, to ward off the Japanese piratical raids on the Yangtsze coasts, had designed a heavily-timbered ship completely shut in—a sort of floating tank—which made it impossible for the dread Japanese swordsmen of those days to board and get to grips with their enemy. The Koreans, whose junk intercourse with China, notably with Shantung and the Liaotung, was constant, had improved on this model and sheathed it with iron scales, making it look like a turtle. To Korea, curiously enough, belongs the honour of using the first ironclads in history; for with a navy composed of such vessels the Korean forces attacked the Japanese transports in Fusan harbour, and at other points along the Korean coast, and almost completely destroyed them. China, on being appealed to, sent army after army to the rescue of her vassal, and although these troops did not greatly distinguish themselves, their dead-weight added to the Korean forces confined the Japanese advance to

GENERAL INTRODUCTION 23

Pingyang—the invaders finally retiring and evacuating Korea in 1598 as a result of their sea-losses and their domestic dissensions. The country had, however, been so terribly ravaged during six long years that it never recovered. The slaughter was so immense that there is shown in Kyoto to this day a mound under which are buried the pickled noses and ears of 35,000 Chinese and Korean troops killed by the clan of Satsuma.

Now, just as the Shogun Yoshimitsu for political purposes had accepted investiture at the hands of a Chinese envoy, so did Hideyoshi after his defeat accept—unknowingly so Japanese historians declare—from the Chinese envoys a document which can have but one meaning. So important is its text as an explanation of the nature of the conflict between the two nations—China claiming a cultural supremacy which Japan constantly rejected by force of arms—that the text should be read:—

> The influence of the holy and divine one (Confucius) is widespread; he is honoured and loved wherever the heavens overhang and the earth upbears. The Imperial command is universal; even as far as the bounds of ocean where the sun rises, there are none who do not obey it.
> In ancient times our Imperial ancestors bestowed their favours on many lands; the Tortoise knots and the Dragon writing were sent to the limits of far Fusang (Japan), the pure alabaster and the great seal character were granted to the mountains of the submissive country. Thereafter came billowy times when communication was interrupted, but an auspicious opportunity has now arrived, when it has pleased us again to address you.
> You, Toyotomi Taira Hideyoshi, having established an Island Kingdom, and knowing the reverence due to the Central land, sent to the West an envoy, and with gladness and affection offered your allegiance. On the North you

knocked at the barrier of ten thousand li, and earnestly requested to be admitted within our dominions. Your mind is already confirmed in reverent submissiveness. How can we grudge our favour to so great meekness ?

We do therefore specially invest you with the dignity of King of Japan, and to that intent issue this our commission. Treasure it up carefully. Over the sea we send you a crown and robe, so that you may follow our ancient custom as respects dress. Faithfully defend the frontier of the Empire ; let it be your study to act worthily of your position as our minister : practise moderation and self-restraint ; cherish gratitude for the Imperial favour so bountifully bestowed upon you ; change not your fidelity ; be humbly guided by our admonitions ; continue always to follow our instructions.

Respect this !

Death, however, prevented Hideyoshi from dealing with a matter of great historical interest. Other influences were at work demanding close attention.

Already, before this turning-point in Far Eastern history, the white man had suddenly appeared on the scenes and by his presence changed the whole course of events.

IV

In 1542 a Portuguese junk on a voyage from Siam to Macao was blown from her course and fetched up off the coasts of Satsuma province. The mariners were well received. Great curiosity was excited by their arquebuses, arms of any sort always delighting the Japanese ; and these arquebuses were rapidly copied and used against the Koreans and the Chinese in the Hideyoshi expedition. The Portuguese sailors carried back the tidings of their discovery with them to their missionaries, the great

Francis de Xavier landing at the chief Satsuma city, Kagoshima, in 1549.

It would take a volume in itself to describe the direct and indirect consequences of the arrival of the European trader and the European priest on Japanese soil. But the net results can be summed up in this way. At first, being desirous of trade, the Christian propagandists were accepted by some of the feudal chiefs, for trade and religion in those days marched hand in hand. A great number of converts were made on the island of Kyushu, and in spite of some friction all was seemingly well. But when the selfsame Hideyoshi in 1587, prior to his Korean expedition, had carried out the subjection of Kiushu and the Satsuma clans, he propounded the following five questions to the Jesuits :—

"Why and by what authority the propagandists had constrained Japanese to become Christian converts ? Why they had induced their disciples to overthrow Buddhist temples ? Why did they persecute the bonzes ? Why they ate animals useful to man ? Why the Jesuit chiefs allowed merchants of their nation to buy Japanese and to make them slaves in the Indies ? "

The reply given to this *questionnaire* was deemed unsatisfactory, and Hideyoshi issued his famous edict of expulsion. For at least ten years considerations of trade prevented the edict from being carried out, but with the coming of Franciscan monks a new phase was reached.

The Franciscans were Spaniards and were rivals of the Portuguese. Established at Manila, where their compatriots carried on a regular trade with Spanish South America, they bitterly disliked the rival order of Jesuits and were determined to humiliate them. The Jesuits, having been placed under a ban, were carrying on their religious observances secretly. The Franciscans scouted their methods. In spite of a Papal bull, which put Japan beyond their scope, they persisted in going into the country, penetrating even to Kyoto, which was then the Imperial residence, and making a number of converts. A purely fortuitous act brought their doom. A Spanish galleon, on her way from Manila to South America, drifted on to the rocks and, being very richly laden, was seized as a prize. The pilot, in a last effort to save his vessel, showed the Japanese officers a map of the world and the vast extent of the Spanish dominions. Asked to explain how one country had acquired such sway, he made the historic reply: " Our kings begin by sending into the countries they wish to conquer missionaries who induce the people to embrace our religion, and when they have made considerable progress, troops are sent to combine with the new Christians, and then our kings have not much trouble in accomplishing the rest."

On learning this speech Hideyoshi was overcome with fury and ordered still more severe measures. He died before his policy was completed, but the Tokugawa Shogun who succeeded him left nothing to be desired on the score of severity. Japan was, however, still torn by civil war, and the foreign question, although urgent, was eclipsed by domestic issues. Consequently, although another edict of expulsion was issued in 1614, i.e. twenty-seven years after Hideyoshi had taken action, and still another in 1616, it was not until 1638 that the final act was played. In that year the last remaining group of

Japanese Christians, numbering it is said 20,000 fighting men and 17,000 women and children, retired to the promontory of Shimabara in the Gulf of Nagasaki. There these insurgents, fighting under flags with red crosses and with battle-cries of Jesus and Maria, were attacked and almost entirely exterminated, and Christianity in Japan disappeared.

In this last act a Dutch trading-vessel had played a part, assisting the Shogun's forces in the bombardment. The Dutch had been granted a license to trade in 1605. They possessed precisely the qualifications suited to the situation then existing in Japan: they had commercial potentialities without any religious associations; and when the Spaniards and Portuguese had been entirely expelled the field was left entirely to them—the island of Deshima in Nagasaki, which was not more than three hundred yards long, being the sole window left open to the world. Every kind of indignity was, however, imposed upon the Dutch. No Dutchman could be buried on Japanese soil. Every Dutch ship had her rudder, guns, and ammunition removed, and her sails sealed, and no religious service of any sort could be held; and this condition of affairs existed for a period of 217 years, until the coming of Perry. Not only this, but no Japanese might build vessels capable of navigating the high seas. The Japanese, foiled in Korea and fearful of the empires of the West, had irrevocably sealed themselves up.

V

There is in all history no such singular *dénouement* to the double policy Hideyoshi had inaugurated.

A complete consolidation of the forces of feudalism now followed the failure of foreign conquest; and it is very important to realize how much all this has affected the character of the Japanese, and how during the last three decades they have attempted to do what they failed to accomplish three centuries ago.

Thrown back on themselves, their innate characteristics became intensified—they became more and more like themselves. With minute and voluminous regulations governing every activity; with the guards of the feudal lords on every highway, making travel from one fief to another impossible save under special license; entirely cut off from the outer world, and having no connection even with Korea save what the Daimyo of Tsushima might do by almost stealth at the tiny Fusan settlement, Japan in the seventeenth and eighteenth centuries was further from China than she was from Europe and America, since the Dutch traders at Deshima were at least a connecting link with the West. There was indeed no single exchange of documents or any species of intercourse between China and Japan from the proclamation of the Manchu dynasty in Peking in 1644 until the commercial treaty of Tientsin of 1871.

It is necessary to consider this matter from a special point of view.

Whilst the Ming emperors did not greatly welcome the first appearance of Western navigators in their seas in 1518—i.e. twenty-six years before they reached Japan—no direct action was taken by them until the savagery of the Portuguese trading-crews and their raids into the country in search of women spread alarm and led to popular reprisals. Then only was intercourse confined to Macao and Canton, and a policy of control inaugurated.

Canton was well fitted to maintain trade relations with unknown nations. Originally founded by Chinese sea-adventurers, who had sailed down the Chinese coasts and forced their way into the small aboriginal kingdoms during the first centuries of the Christian era, it had not been formally incorporated in the Empire until the T'ang dynasty (A.D. 618–907). In the eighth and ninth centuries the spread of Islamism had brought Arab navigators to the uttermost East, and soon Chinese vessels, although generally going not further than the Malacca Straits, journeyed as far as Africa and the Indies. Marco Polo himself at the end of the thirteenth century, when he left the land of Cathay after his remarkable sojourn at the Court of Kublai Khan, sailed from Amoy, in the southern province of Fuhkien, for the Persian Gulf in a Chinese deep-sea junk, of which he says:—

> And first let us speak of the ships in which merchants go to and fro amongst the Isles of India. These ships, you must know, are of fir timber. They have but one deck, though each of them contains some fifty or sixty cabins wherein the merchants abide greatly at their ease, every man having one to himself. The ship hath but one rudder, but it hath four masts; and sometimes they have two additional masts, which they ship and unship at pleasure. Each of these great ships requires at least 200 mariners, some of them 300. They are indeed of great size; for one ship shall carry 5,000 or 6,000 baskets of pepper, and they used to be formerly larger than they are now. . . .

The Cantonese and other South Chinese were therefore very familiar with foreign things; their argosies had long dotted the seas of the Malay archipelago when the first *conquistadores* passed through the Malacca Straits and reached out for the Yellow seas; and until atrocities and arquebuses became synonymous terms the fair-faced foreigners were not restricted.

Here we have in a single sentence the history of two centuries of Euro-Chinese intercourse. The traders of Canton were not like the historic burghers of Calais who were forced to surrender the keys of their city to an alien conqueror : they merely adapted themselves to the exigencies of the hour and secured a trade monopoly by inaugurating and stereotyping a mercantile system which greatly resembled the system of medieval Europe. The emporia at Canton and at the adjacent port of Macao completely supplied the wants of buyers and sellers : in China, unlike Japan, there was no fear of foreign conquest —restriction was simply a police measure.

In religion as in commerce there is much the same story. Matteo Ricci, the first Jesuit to establish himself in China, came to Canton in 1581 and reached Peking twenty years later. He was then an accomplished Chinese scholar, and was duly presented to the Ming emperor Wan Li, who greatly welcomed him. When the Manchu cavalry entered Peking in 1644 as a result of treachery at the Great Wall and the Mings disappeared, the Jesuit Fathers were so firmly entrenched and had so many thousands of converts that they were fully accepted by the new dynasty—just as the Greek Patriarchate was accepted by the Turks after the conquest of Constantinople. It was a question of national discipline, ancestor-worship, which finally brought conflict, the rival monastic orders of the Franciscans and the Dominicans refusing to accept the complaisance of the Jesuits and calling the practice idolatry. The matter was referred to the Popes and there were conflicting rulings. In the year 1700 the great emperor Kang Hsi definitely proclaimed that "the customs of China are political"—meaning that ancestor-worship was part of the national discipline and must be maintained; and although the Popes dissented and hurled anathemas at all who tolerated the practice, it was not until 1724—that is, after a century and a half of close religious intercourse—that an edict of expulsion was issued in Peking and only partially obeyed. The early nineteenth century indeed found Catholic missionaries still working in China in secret, and they were the first Europeans to penetrate Korea. They were indeed part and parcel of the external forces which were forcing open China, and when the first Japanese treaty of 1871 was signed with China, missionaries of all denominations had been commonplaces for two generations.

VI

Adequately to treat this critical period of history—the renewal of direct and formal intercourse between China and Japan late in the nineteenth century, as a result of the opening of the two countries by the military action of the West—requires what is entirely missing, namely, a critical and authentic monograph on the statesman Li Hung Chang, who, until the outbreak of the war over Korea in 1894, so largely controlled the foreign relations of Peking. We do not yet know the things we require to know; we are still in the dark. The handling of evidence, the assignment of proportion, the testing of policy—all these things, difficult enough in the case of Western statesmen, become doubly so when Oriental statecraft is mixed with European issues, and the whole hidden in the twilight of an old-fashioned Yamen. Brought in 1870 to the gateway of the capital (for Tientsin is the gateway to Peking) as metropolitan viceroy and High Commissioner for Trade in the Northern Seas, Li Hung Chang had behind him all the prestige he had won by crushing, with General Gordon's aid, the last despairing efforts of the Taiping rebels. It was his particular duty to contrive machinery to resist foreign pressure; to limit international intercourse to the coastline; and thus to prevent clashes between an ignorant proletariat and a defiant mercantilism. Already the foundations of the Chinese State had been so sapped by internal discontent and external attacks that very little more was required to bring irreparable dynastic disaster. Japan was then a very small issue: but Korea, infallibly and inevitably, provided the meeting-place for the inherent rivalry between two nations.

In 1868 Japan had informed the Seoul Government of the restoration of the Meiji emperor through the intermediary of the Daimyo of Tsushima; but her demands for an acknowledgment of vassalage had been peremptorily rejected. War might even then have come had it not been for the wisdom of the statesmen of the Restoration period. The persistent efforts of the Western maritime Powers to enter into trade relations with the Hermit Kingdom had filled the coasts of Korea with alarm almost from the beginning of the nineteenth century, and had culminated in the United States sending in 1871 a special mission. But the American gunboats had been fired upon, and a sharp action had ensued which had resulted in Korean coast forts being captured and destroyed. This gesture was, however, fruitless, and another decade passed before Western diplomacy intervened again. China was apparently indifferent ; to this day no one accurately knows whether she foresaw what must soon occur.

On Japan, however, American action in Korea had an immediate and powerful repercussion ; it was borne in on her that not one day should be wasted in delay. Nearly thirty years had now passed since China had been opened by foreign treaties ; nearly twenty since she herself had given effect to Perry's demands. Yet China and Japan were officially not cognizant of each other's existence, and were unrepresented at each other's Court.

In the autumn of 1871 (i.e four months after the American gunboat affair off Chemulpo) Date, the Japanese Minister of Foreign Affairs, arrived in Tientsin and signed with Li Hung Chang a treaty which materially and radically differed from all other treaties China had made. Its language and its clauses have indeed to-day the highest importance ; for they reveal the fact that the first attempt of Japan to accommodate herself to a type of relationship alien and antithetical to Eastern culture was made in a spirit of equality. The written, precise agreement, which Europe owes to Roman Law, here appears in flowing, ceremonious language ; and what should have been from its very nature clearly and absolutely defined from the very beginning is only vaguely touched upon.

Listen to the language.

Article I declares :—

Henceforth the friendship between China and Japan shall be increased and shall last like heaven and earth forever. The countries subject to each state shall in like manner treat each other with respect, and shall commit no acts of hostility towards each other, to the end that everlasting peace may be maintained.

Article II declares :—

Now that friendly relations subsist between the two countries, this friendship shall without fail be of an intimate and reciprocal character. Should either state experience at the hands of another country injustice or slighting treatment, on communication being made to the other state the latter shall give assistance or shall use her good offices in mediating between the two countries. Thus friendship shall be increased.

Article III declares :—

The system of administration and the laws of the two countries being different, each country shall be free to conduct its own administration independently. Neither country shall be permitted to interfere in the concerns of the other and press for the adoption of things prohibited by law. Assistance shall be rendered mutually for the enforcement of laws, and each country shall give orders to its merchants that they must not lead astray the people of the other country or commit any offence whatsoever.

Was there any discussion, it may be asked, about Korea or did both plenipotentiaries avoid the issue? No one knows, for the treaty-makers are dead—and their diaries have been destroyed.

GENERAL INTRODUCTION 85

But even more interesting than these general political maxims, in which the two sovereign states dimly take cognizance of each other's existence, are the two articles which *give each country extraterritorial rights at ports open to trade where consuls have been stationed, and failing that leave control in the hands of local officials who are authorized to execute justice after lex loci.* China (and the fact has capital importance to-day) possessed in the period 1871–94 limited extraterritorial rights in Japan precisely as Japan possessed limited extraterritorial rights in China—and it was this question just as much as the question of Korea which ultimately made an attack on China necessary to Japan.

Article VIII declares :—

Each country shall, in each of the ports of the other country which are open to trade, station a Consul who will exercise control over the merchants of his nationality. All matters relating to property of all kinds, to business or professions, and to judicial suits, shall be referred for settlement to the Consul, who shall decide them according to the laws of his country. Suits arising between merchants of the two countries shall be brought in the form of petitions; the Consul shall endeavour to settle such cases, and shall do his utmost to prevent them being made the subject of litigation. When a settlement cannot be effected in this manner, the Consul shall act in accordance with justice. In cases of robbery and absconding (where the aggrieved party is an alien), it will be sufficient for the local authorities of each country to arrest the offenders and take back the stolen property; the Government concerned shall in no case be required to make compensation.

Article IX declares :—

Should in any open port of either country no Consul be appointed, the local authorities of the country in question shall exercise control over the subjects and trade of the other country, and render good offices; should an offence be committed, they shall arrest and try the offender, and after reporting the facts of the case to the Consul at the nearest open port, give sentence according to the law.

By one of those curious ironies which are not rare in history, within three months of its signature the treaty was subjected to an acid test by an incident in the Loochoo Islands. This string of islands, which forms a pendent to the islands of Japan, was for centuries tributary both to China and Japan. But China was the older suzerain. Tribute was first sent to China in A.D. 1372 and to Japan only in 1451. The princes of the Loochoos had also received their investiture regularly from the emperors of China since the time of the Ming sovereign Yung Lo (1403-25); but the islands had been conquered by the Prince of Satsuma in 1609, and since that date their princes had received investiture from the emperor of Japan. When in 1871 some Loochoo Islanders were shipwrecked on the coast of Formosa and killed and eaten by the head-hunters of the mountains, Japan demanded redress for her subjects, and China made no counter-claim of suzerainty. Li Hung Chang, however, accepted responsibility and undertook the chastisement of the Formosan savages; but his decision was almost immediately reversed by the Peking Government, which declared that the tribes in question acknowledged no overlord. Japan then dispatched an expedition of 3,000 troops—which caused the Chinese Government once again to change its policy, and claim the sole right to intervene in Formosan affairs. Chinese troops were likewise sent to Formosa and the two countries

GENERAL INTRODUCTION 37

seemed to be drifting into war; the intervention of the British envoy in Peking effected a settlement by means of an indemnity. The language of the settlement recorded in Peking on the 31st October, 1874, is important because it was signed by the great Japanese statesman Okubo, who had long specialized in his country's foreign relations. The preamble says :—

... Certain Japanese subjects having been wantonly murdered by the unreclaimed savages of Formosa, the Government of Japan regarding these savages as responsible dispatched a force against them to exact satisfaction. An understanding has now been come to with the Government of China that this force shall be withdrawn and certain steps taken ; all of which is set forth in the three Articles following.

Thus Japan assumes successfully that the people of a principality tributary to both China and Japan are Japanese subjects. This principle, once asserted, henceforth guided all her policy in her contest with her great neighbour.

VII

In 1875 some Japanese sailors were fired upon from the Korean forts which the Americans had destroyed four years previously. Once again the forts were levelled and Japan informed China of her intentions. It was not only Chinese claims which were irritating to her, but the menace of Russian arms was keenly felt. Not only had Russia, by the use of chicanery, annexed in 1860 the whole Pacific province of Manchuria and founded the great city of Vladivostok, but she had attempted in 1861 to do what the Mongols under Kublai Khan had done—to occupy the strategic island of Tsushuma, which commands the Korean Straits. China gave Korea friendly advice regarding the establishment of amicable relations, but although Japan sent a dispatch to the Seoul Court proposing a treaty it was rejected. In February 1876 an ambassador and a divisional general, with the necessary troops, anchored off Korea prepared for peace or war—and a treaty resulted, characteristically signed by the divisional general, in which the independence of Korea was acknowledged.

What did this signify? How was it possible to reconcile such a declaration with the tribute missions which still regularly proceeded to Peking, and which were a matter of common knowledge? Did it mean that the new-type relationship which Western arms had forced on Eastern empires—with written Roman Law agreements—must inevitably destroy old cultural claims and the old hegemony? No one knows, but it is not mere coincidence that in the year following this treaty Li Hung Chang should have annexed to China the forty-mile neutral strip on the west, or Chinese, bank of the Yalu River, which for centuries had been a No-man's-land, because it lay beyond the old boundary palisade. Plainly the move showed fear—a dim realization that a "strategic frontier" was being menaced.

Yet in spite of these things there seems to have been no definite policy regarding the main factor —foreign pressure. In 1881, however, Li Hung Chang wrote a dispatch to the Korean Court advising

GENERAL INTRODUCTION

" limited treaties " with the Western Powers. In 1882 the United States, still hankering after proper relations, sent a commodore on board of an American gunboat escorted by three Chinese men-of-war; and precisely as Commodore Perry had done a generation before in Tokio Bay, finally signed the first Western treaty.

Immediately after this event we get an important clue. The American treaty had been signed in May: in September Chinese and Korean officials, meeting at Tientsin, come to a written agreement and disclose in a single sentence the real nature of the relationship existing between China and Korea. The preamble to " the Regulations for maritime and overland trade between Chinese and Korean subjects of 1882 " begins in this way :—

> . . . All that pertains to the relations of Korea as a boundary state of China has been long ago regulated by fixed rules, and no change is required in this respect. But as now foreign countries entertain trade with Korea by water, it becomes necessary to remove at once the prohibition of sea trade hitherto enforced between China and Korea, and let the merchants of both countries participate in all the advantages of commercial relations ; the regulations affecting the exchange of produce on the frontier will also, as time may require, be modified ; but the new regulations for the maritime and overland trade now decided upon are understood to apply to the relations between China and Korea only, the former country granting to the latter certain advantages as a tributary kingdom, and treaty nations are not to participate therein. It is in this sense that the following Articles have been agreed upon.

At last we see clearly. Korea was a " boundary state " precisely as Annam, Tonking, Siam, Burmah, Tibet, Nepaul, Eastern Turkestan, and the Principalities of Outer Mongolia were boundary states, i.e. buffer territories ruled over by lesser kings. Surrounding the ancient Middle Kingdom, which was looked upon as centre of all things because in the Confucian cosmogony the emperors, Sons of Heaven, were necessarily the High Priests of all who acknowledged the sway of Chinese culture, they had a definite and special rôle to fulfil. It is easy to see that the difficulties facing China in the nineteenth century were the difficulties facing England in India, where for the same reasons, although they were given another name, the Russian advance in Central Asia, which was leading to the absorption of the independent Khanates, menaced the whole buffer-territory theory. China's predicament in Korea was therefore England's predicament in Afghanistan; intercourse by water had been absolutely and rigidly cut off even between suzerain and tributary because the only method of enforcing a veto in the East is to make it absolute. Westernism, of which Japan had become a pretended exponent, was destructive of the old sanction. Water was the element which could not be controlled. It is water to-day which still remains the master-force in the Far East. . . .

In 1883 further regulations to control Korean frontier traffic throw further light on an obscure and difficult subject. Chinese and Korean officials, talking to one another in the Liaotung, reveal some of the curiosities of the old relationship. One clause states that "it being one of the prerogatives of the Court of China to draw its supply of fish for sacrificial purposes from the embouchures of rivers situated on the Chinese side of the Yalu and in the Korean district of Pingyang, the people are strictly forbidden to fish there clandestinely." What visions of a long departed past does this not conjure up, the Altar of Heaven and the Temple of Imperial Ancestors in Peking, so many hundreds of miles away, drawing supplies by prescriptive right from this tributary region! Another clause declares just as unemotionally : " Whereas all the territory under the jurisdiction of the Liaotung is Crown land attached to His Majesty's Second Capital and subject to the rules which formerly received Imperial sanction, merchants who come for the purchase of local produce can only be allowed, whether coming or going, to pass through the sidegates of the Fenghuang palisade passage ; travellers who have been turned back from the tribute-road must not choose roads according to their fancy."

How redolent of the seventeenth century! For " His Majesty's Second Capital " is Moukden— the original chief city of the little Manchu principality which after fifty years of struggle had captured Peking. And just as miniatures or skeletons of the great Boards of State are maintained even to this day in Hsianfu, which ceased to be the national capital thirteen centuries ago, so was Moukden still spoken of as " the second capital." And the palisade which appears so casually—forty miles from the Yalu River—is the old Chinese boundary palisade built by the Ming dynasty in the fifteenth century to protect Chinese settlers from Manchu raids—where guards were still maintained in ignorance of the old purpose.

By these marks we see something of tragedy

which Westernism, sweeping in by the sea, spelt for an old-world empire.

Meanwhile in the capital of Korea this upsetting of the time-honoured past was provoking as desperate a struggle as it had in Japan during the last days of the Tokugawa Shogunate; the Korean royal family, torn by intrigues, was divided into a so-called conservative pro-Chinese party, led by the ill-fated Queen, and a so-called liberal pro-Japanese party. The destruction of the Japanese Legation and the general mob-violence, induced by the signing of the first foreign treaties in 1882, culminated in the landing of Yuan Shih-kai and other generals with 3,000 Chinese troops to back up the Queen's party. And these were promptly followed by the landing of the same number of Japanese troops.

This meeting of China and Japan face to face after centuries of isolation filled the air with electricity. Instinctively the two nations hated one another. All the jealousy and bad blood of generations seemed to be concentrated in Seoul, and incident followed incident with bewildering rapidity. In 1884 several thousand Korean and Chinese troops under Yuan Shih-kai attacked one of the palaces which was defended by two companies of Japanese infantry. More Chinese and Japanese troops arrive and rumours of war grow. But the pear was not yet ripe; and accordingly in 1885 the late Prince Ito proceeds to Tientsin and signs yet another convention with Li Hung Chang.

In this instrument China and Japan mutually undertake to evacuate Korea: they declare that they "shall respectively accomplish the withdrawal of the whole number of each of their troops, in order to avoid effectively any complications between the two countries: the Chinese troops shall embark from Asan; and the Japanese from the port of Chemulpo." They also undertake not to send troops without giving prior notice. But regarding the essential issue, the definition of the true status of Korea, neither is yet ready to commit itself, although in an additional clause they "mutually agree to invite the King of Korea to instruct and drill a sufficient armed force, that she may herself assure her public security, and to invite him to engage into his service an officer or officers from amongst those of a third Power who shall be entrusted with the instruction of the said force."

Following this, American officers arrive and drill Korean troops for a brief space; and England, after a few more months, evacuates Port Hamilton, which she had occupied because Russia seemed about to move south to the "warm water." But the real issue is Yuan Shih-kai and the policy of Tientsin. This man, later to aspire to the throne of China, had returned to Seoul as Imperial Resident—having induced Li Hung Chang to consent to this cunning step because Japan only possessed a Minister Plenipotentiary.

And so at last the storm is there on the horizon-line, plainly to be seen by those with vision.

VIII

China, after the lesson of the Tonkin war with France (1884–85), had commenced the fortification of Port Arthur under Li Hung Chang's guidance.

She likewise vastly improved her navy, which soon included two ironclads and a number of good cruisers, placing the whole under the joint command of a Chinese admiral and a British admiral. But in 1890 the Englishman lost his post as the result of a petty dispute—and China's fate in Korea was sealed. Corruption and inefficiency soon reigned supreme in the new navy, which might have repeated the performance of the Korean armoured ships of the sixteenth century, but which went into action in 1894 at the Battle of the Yalu with sand-filled shells, and so changed all history.

Japan's determination to wage war against China came in 1894—immediately she had signed her treaty with Britain abolishing extraterritoriality in Japan. War was held by her a necessary step not only to consummate her international emancipation but to take from China rights which embarrassed her. The facts that follow have supreme importance to-day.

The British treaty abolishing extraterritoriality was signed on the 16th July, 1894, when events in Korea, due to the so-called Tong Hak rebellion, had led to the landing of both Chinese and Japanese troops. The first act of war, the sinking of the chartered transport "Kowshing" carrying Chinese reinforcements by a Japanese cruiser, did not occur until the 25th July, i.e. until nine days after the treaty had duly been signed in London. In other words, Japan was working by time-table on the accepted Prussian model. Land-fighting was delayed until three days later, Japan only issuing her declaration of war on 1st August, having on the 28rd July broken into, and taken possession of, the royal palace and carried off the Queen and her children, which allowed her to appoint a puppet Regent.

The rest of the Powers quickly followed England's example in the manner of extraterritoriality, and in her greatly improved position among the nations it was essential for Japan *that the privileges of extraterritoriality in China—which she did not then possess on the same basis as the Western powers—should be acquired by her, whilst the limited extraterritorial jurisdiction China possessed in Japan should be forcibly cancelled.*

This is one of the deeper reasons for Japanese action in Korea. Although China agreed to the complete independence of Korea almost after her first defeats, Japan was aiming at very different objects. The cession of the Liaotung, or the area included in the old willow palisade, *plus* the annexed Yalu zone, was but one small thing, just as Formosa was another. The real prize was the reversal of the old relationship between China and Japan— that suzerain China should become the tributary and tributary Japan the suzerain. Everything else is subordinate to this root-idea. The intervention of Russia and her satellites in 1895, which was followed by the brutal Japanese murder of the Korean Queen and the loss of all Japanese influence, and then by the Manchurian war—these and many other things are but interruptions in the grand policy—interruptions due to necessity and to world-influence. The root-idea to-day, as it has been for many years, is to complete the plan of making suzerain China the tributary and tributary Japan the suzerain. The so-called Far Eastern Monroe

Doctrine, which the Tokyo Government has fitfully tried to propagate, is nothing but a new covering to mask the root-idea.

The curious and intricate character of this crisis which necessitates a double policy—one for the West and another for the East—is adequately illustrated in the four chapters that follow.

CHAPTER II

THE OUTLINE OF THE FAR EAST

THE writer can lay claim to an intimate knowledge of the Far East and of everything that affects it. Almost his earliest memory of childhood is of a great crowd of many thousands of shouting men, stripped to the waist, and armed with bamboo carriers' poles, who had swarmed forward determined to destroy the house of his father because five square black characters on the door-plate proclaimed that it was the official residence of a commissioner—one responsible for the levying of taxes. The salt-tax had just been raised, to pay for the Tonkin war of 1884; and these men, coming on shore from the great fleet of salt-junks which were tied up along miles of the Yangtsze River, were trying to secure a remission by intimidation. Characteristically, they were threatening the wrong authority; but long experience had taught them that in a country of compromises violence of any sort is effective as a political argument, and that it is better to hit the wrong man rather than no man at all. . . . That was the curious Chinese question thrusting itself on his immature attention, a vast question in many ways, yet nevertheless inherently simple, since it is made up of the crudest economic problems, which have not changed throughout the ages.

Since those days of thirty-seven years ago a good deal of water has flowed under the bridges and a good many changes have come. War, and war's alarms, were responsible a quarter of a century ago for the handing over of China to the international money-lender. With indebtedness came complications and irritations. The year 1900 was signalized by that big "blow-out" called the Boxer rising; and the settlement which followed was still further complicated by the complete breakdown in 1905 of the fiction of Russian invincibility which had so obsessed the late Lord Salisbury and the present Lord Lansdowne during the periods when they controlled British Foreign policy, that to it alone must be traced most of the disasters of our own hectic decade. The fabric of Far Eastern relations having been based on balance-of-power, which is only another name for a refusal to face the inevitable, the declension of Russia destroyed the patchwork scheme, and made one of two things certain—that either China must win her complete independence or be carved up.

In 1911 a valiant attempt was made on the part of Young China to secure the first alternative by erecting a republic. But, as the writer has sought to explain in another work,[1] the attempt was not a great success mainly because the liberal Powers of the world, being every whit as short-sighted then as they have shown themselves in the case of Russia, did not love the Chinese Revolution— only tolerating the elimination of the Manchu autocracy because the foreign bondholders' interest in the country was not directly affected. At the earliest possible opportunity they assisted reaction in the person of Yuan Shih-kai; subsidized him so that

[1] *The Fight for the Republic in China.*

he might destroy all his rivals and the embryo of parliamentary government into the bargain; and then were mightily surprised that he should have aspired to a burlesque kingship which killed him and left the country pretty well wrecked.

The results of the republican experiment in China, so far as Europe was concerned, were thus counted quite negligible. It was said by professional diplomats, who probably know less about politics than any other body of men, and who have been badly frightened all the world over by the rise of popular power, that the Chinese were not fit for self-government, whatever they may mean; and so when President Li Yuan-hung assumed office in the summer of 1916 the Powers had nothing left in the way of a reconstructive plan excepting to induce China to enter the war, hoping that this act would tide things over, and serve to mask five years' discreditable diplomacy. On 14th August, 1917, China did declare war on the Teutonic Powers—being speeded to take that decision by Viscount Ishii's special mission to the United States, which it was feared had sinister objects. But the Chinese declaration was stripped of half its international significance because the country was once more at war with itself—North facing South, and each side declaring that the other was a rebel and seeking by force of arms to subdue it. And as this kind of provincial militarism has become just as much the enemy in China as in Europe, it is well carefully to consider it.

The modern army of China is the child of the collapse of 1900. It is true that prior to the Boxer explosion a few " model " divisions had already been organized as a result of the disastrous Japanese war of 1894–95. There was, for instance, one division of Northern troops under a General Nieh which, although the fact has never been properly chronicled, fought with the utmost gallantry against the international armies around Tientsin, advancing against entrenched positions until it was almost entirely destroyed. There were also some well-trained troops at Nanking and Hankow, and above all there was Yuan Shih-kai's picked division in Shantung.

It was this division which was the germ of the modern Chinese army. When the fugitive Empress Dowager Tsu Hsi and the Emperor Kwang Hsu returned to Peking from far-off Hsianfu in 1902, and sanctioned Yuan Shih-kai's scheme for a National Army, events marched so rapidly—for Asia at least—that by 1905 Yuan Shih-kai as viceroy of the metropolitan province of Chihli and chief of the Army Board was able to hold army manœuvres in which 100,000 well-trained men participated.

At the time this created a great sensation: it was felt by all far-seeing men that Yuan Shih-kai was deliberately raising a force to take the place of the Eight Banners, or Manchu army-corps, which had been the means of effecting the Manchu conquest of China in the seventeenth century, and whose organization—on paper—survived, although the men were entirely worthless and unequipped. Japan, who had just beaten Russia in her Manchurian war, began to realize anew that China was not really a negligible quantity, and that given an army and navy of even moderate efficiency China could re-establish the Far Eastern situation which had existed prior to the Korean war of 1894. The writer believes that a portion of the astonishing diplomatic

THE OUTLINE OF THE FAR EAST 51

story which has been enacted in Peking in the period 1914–18 is due to this one fact—namely, the Japanese fear of a militant China.

Had the revolution of 1911 not created an interregnum, the modern Chinese army would have reached its full authorized establishment (thirty-six field divisions with a peace-footing of half a million men and a war-footing of something over a million) at about the time of the commencement of the World War. But the revolution broke up the reorganization scheme long before it was completed; mixed the old-style and the new troops; and by lowering the standard and introducing politics into the army destroyed unity and discipline.

What Gambetta found in clericalism republican China indeed soon discovered in her militarists. The army, reinforced by myriads of men who had managed to acquire firearms, was plainly the enemy; for the soldiers openly declared that they had made the revolution, and that without them the revolutionary leaders could not have lived an hour. This was unfortunately only half the truth, and therefore as dangerous as all half-truths inherently are. For the revolution was as much the work of the foreigner as it was of the Chinese. The Manchus could never have been dethroned had their borrowing-power on foreign markets not been deliberately cancelled by the action of foreign diplomacy, which yielding to the clamour of publicists declared that the Western world would maintain strict neutrality until a decision was reached. Consequently, the army in spite of its boast was really dependent on an alien paymaster who could only be reached by a method which its leader and creator—Yuan Shih-kai—had brought to a fine art. This method was a mixture of bluff, promises to rival legations, and threats—above all, threats that if hard cash were not forthcoming all China would go up in flames. By finding the monthly quotas for the troops Yuan Shih-kai became supreme.

Only on the surface, however. For the army had become contumacious even before the Manchus had abdicated. Its Northern leaders, roughly grouped together under the name of the Peiyang Party—*Anglice*, the party of the Northern seas or, better, the Northern vice-royalties—had nearly all risen from humble captaincies in Yuan Shih-kai's original model corps (organized in 1896 after the Korean war) to divisional commands; and one and all they coveted the direct control of provinces. In other words, the revolution, having abolished the viceroys, who had ruled over single or linked provinces, and substituted the *Tu-tuh* (now *Tuchun*) or military governor for each province, the aim of all these men was to rule at the provincial capitals where provincial taxation was centred and where money necessarily was to be found.

By the use of terrorist methods, which commenced in Peking on the memorable 29th February, 1912, when the capital was sacked by the Third Division, these divisional commanders soon became the most solid factors in the very fluid *post*-revolutionary China. Commander after commander received as reward for fealty to Yuan Shih-kai the gift of a provincial capital; and although a parliament or assembly of some kind has been in session in Peking most of the time, such real power as there has been since 1911 has been divided among these men.

Nevertheless, the idea of constitutionalism—and the necessity of civil rule being made supreme—has never perished. That idea is stronger to-day than it has ever been before—it is the goal all educated Chinese in their hearts are determined to attain. And because civil rule as opposed to militarism is the proclaimed object of the South-Western group of revolting provinces with their capital at Canton, let us see precisely how the matter stands.

The struggle between North and South in China is very old. In one form or another it has gone on for eight hundred years—in fact ever since the Kitan and Chin Tartars burst through the Great Wall in the eleventh and twelfth centuries and commenced the Tartar military supremacy in North China which has so profoundly modified the old Chinese ritual of government. For although the Ming dynasty (Chinese) broke the Mongol supremacy, and moved the capital from Nanking to Peking five hundred years ago, the Mings were soon enough ousted by the Manchus (Tartars again), who stereotyped nearly three centuries ago the conception of a military domination directed from Peking—a domination which, no matter how unreal it may have become, still lives in Northern China as a political concept, tradition playing such a powerful rôle among the educated and uneducated alike that no amount of argument can kill it. This, then, is the real quarrel between North and South, in spite of all talk about constitutionalism—namely, that the Peking tradition of a military domination has not been killed and cannot be killed until universal education has definitely relegated it to the limbo of forgotten things.

From the beginning of the revolution—that is, from October 1911—the Northern army was not only filled with this tradition but was conscious of its strength. A number of the Northern provinces had so far completed their reorganization that Yuan Shih-kai at the time of the Manchu abdication had certainly a quarter of a million fairly well-found troops under his direct orders. South of the Yangtsze the situation was very different. Some provinces had no more than mixed brigades of reorganized troops; and although five Southern provinces—Hupeh, Kiangsi, Chekiang, Kwangtung, and Yunnan—could each muster at least one good modern division with artillery and transport, they were without proper arsenals and were vastly outnumbered by swarms of old levies. Moreover, all the machinery of army administration, as well as all the reserves of arms and ammunition, were under the control of Peking; and when we add that the borrowing power had been inherited by those who were ten minutes from Legation Street, it will be seen that the odds could not but be heavily in favour of the North.

Nevertheless, the South remained determined regarding the necessity of substituting effective parliamentary government for military dictation. The Southern leaders, of course, knew that they had not really won in 1912 when the infant emperor Hsuan-Tung abdicated, and that the big battle had yet to be fought. The abdication had been due primarily to Yuan Shih-kai, who was influenced by three things—hatred of a dynasty that had desired his blood; ambition to rule the nation himself; and an inveterate habit of following foreign opinion because that opinion controlled the stock markets on which China had lived for twenty years. Consequently, when the Manchus had been eliminated, there remained for him two controlling impulses and only two—his ambition and the foreign money-market. Everything else —parliament, people, and provincial capitals—was for him mere shadow-play and not reality. It is only when the problem is thus envisaged that what took place can be understood.

In the spring of 1913, i.e. considerably more than a year later than it should have occurred, the first republican parliament with a large Southern majority met in Peking in spite of the assassination of their leader Sung Chiaojen at Shanghai under Yuan Shih-kai's orders. Not only was there this majority, but by virtue of the provisional constitution, which was the law of the land, the Southern leaders believed that they could effectively control Yuan Shih-kai by reducing him to a figurehead. Quickly disillusionized by his signature without parliamentary endorsement of the great Reorganization Loan, which gave him the one thing he needed to secure open mastery—money—they nevertheless held to their point for several months, only inciting open rebellion in the end because they saw that force was still the sole argument.

This trumpery affair of July and August 1913, commonly called the Second Revolution, which was over in a few weeks, thanks to the military strength of the North, further weakened the South by allowing the Northern divisional generals, who had hitherto not been in office south of the Yangtsze, to occupy the whole line of provincial capitals running from

Wuchang (Hankow) to the sea. By the end of the revolt the North was therefore considerably stronger than it had been in 1912. Not only were fourteen out of twenty-one provinces openly in its hand—forming a solid block of territory from the Amur to a point south of Shanghai—but portions of the remaining seven provinces were menaced, making the Southern outlook as black as it could be.

Had Yuan Shih-kai not abandoned himself to the last of the three impulses which had dictated his entire policy from 1911—his ambition—he would possibly be alive to-day as ruler of a very centralized and very bureaucratic commonwealth. But in 1915, yielding to the importunities of his family circle and of his friends—who declared that the moment had arrived for the substitution of a legalized régime for his *de facto* dictatorship—he gave his consent for the monarchy movement, and thereby signed his death-warrant.

There is even to-day a controversy among scholars as to precisely why there should have been such a pother about his attempting to do what so many Chinese had successfully done in their four thousand years of written history. From the beginning of time—that is, from the days of Yao and Shun, who are said to have flourished long before the Tartar shepherd kings, the Hyksos, invaded Egypt (2000 B.C.)—Chinese citizens have been upsetting old dynasties and making new ones. The right which the early emperors had of nominating anyone they pleased as successor—the doctrine of the blood royal being unknown—was held to be good warrant for an illustrious minister mounting the Dragon Throne, the Imperial yellow signifying a priestship rather than a military kingship. Yuan Shih-kai's friends indeed declared that really constitutional monarchy, in which Chinese thought and Western political thought would be impartially mixed, would kill the Tartar-military taint attaching to Peking, and bring national contentment. But his enemies retorted that not only was his sanction of such a scheme deliberate treachery—and the revelations since made regarding the so-called national referendum certainly disclosed unblushing fraud—but that what he aimed at was simply the selfsame family rule, with all its corruption and sycophancy made ten times worse with the help of well-trained men—who would have the skill of scientific criminals. Moreover, those in touch with political life were assured that since Yuan Shih-kai had rejected the Japanese protectorate which Mr. Hioki, the Japanese plenipotentiary, had offered him at the time of the Twenty-one Demands (18th January, 1915), Japan would certainly defeat his plan by hook or crook. Consequently, the outbreak of the so-called Third Revolution on Christmas Day, 1915, this time not on the Yangtsze but in the inaccessible province of Yunnan, foreshadowed his fall, since even the Northern generals refused to support him generally.

On the 6th June, 1916, Yuan Shih-kai died a broken-hearted man. The South once more was jubilant, declaring that at last it had won. But in 1916, as in 1912, it was not really a victory for the Southern party: it was a qualified victory for certain Southern military leaders in certain Southern provinces, Tsai-ao, the brilliant young Yunnan leader, who had done all the fighting, dying before he could consolidate his gains and make his weight really felt. Vice-President Li Yuan-hung, who now assumed office as President, although a thoroughly honest man, was a mere hostage in Peking without a single soldier from his native province of Hupeh to support him. It required the revolt of the whole navy to force the Northern military party to agree even to the restoration of the provisional Constitution and the re-convocation of the dissolved Parliament of 1913; and, therefore, under the surface, when Parliament reassembled it was simply the situation of 1913 over again, *minus* Yuan Shih-kai. When the war-issue came up early in 1917, owing to America's invitation to China to join in the battle against submarine piracy, the question of the permanent Constitution had already nearly wrecked Parliament, the Southern majority not being sufficient to force through the vital clauses. Consequently, just as Yuan Shih-kai had used the signature of the great Reorganization Loan to break the power of Parliament in 1913, so in 1917 the Northern Party began to use the question of a declaration of war against Germany as an intimidation against the majority party, being greatly fortified by the attitude of the Allied legations, who so greatly desired that step to be taken that everything else was held immaterial.

Thereupon began an extraordinary struggle. President Li Yuan-hung seemed to have it in his hands not only to settle the constitutional question by a display of firmness but to define once and for all China's foreign policy. But, being without competent help and without troops, his nerve failed him at the psychological moment; and illegally he dissolved Parliament after diplomatic relations with Germany had been broken off, but before any

THE OUTLINE OF THE FAR EAST

formal declaration of war had been made. At the same time adding folly to his great mistake, he had called to Peking the illiterate General Chang Hsün, who carried out a burlesque restoration of the Manchus —a mockery which was dissipated by a brief fusillade. The result was to leave North and South worse divided than ever; the Northern military party being once more in firm control of Peking, whilst the fugitive Southerners were once more forced back to the home of the Revolution—Canton. For several years the situation has continued like that, with fitful fighting along the northern edge of the seven south-western provinces, and with the foreign Powers looking on helplessly and wondering whether it would ever end.

Whilst the expression "the foreign Powers" is still in general use to signify the whole group of nations in treaty relations with China, recent events have proved that the proper way of expressing foreign political activities should be "the foreign Powers and Japan." For although Japan is an ally of the Allies, and although since her first treaty of alliance with England in 1902, in which Chinese integrity was so carefully guaranteed, she has repeatedly exchanged agreements, notes, secret memoranda, and what not with half the Powers of Christendom, affirming the selfsame principles, her Chinese policy is as purely a Japanese product as are the *geta* (wooden clogs) of the Japanese people. That policy clatters noisily along the international highroad just as if it were shod in resonant *geta* so that everyone can see and hear it; but every so often the clogs are slipped off and Japan enters her neighbour's house in her stockinged feet (as good manners demand); and then very secretly behind the *shoji* (screens) she whispers that unless her tutelage is accepted it will be highly unfortunate for China.

It would be mere repetition of things already outlined to re-examine the problem of the Chinese Revolution from the Japanese standpoint. But this at least ought to be said : that nothing which has occurred in the Far East since the Perry expedition of sixty years ago has more disconcerted Japan than the institution of republicanism at her very doors. Having with vast difficulty and trouble adjusted her national life to the requirements of the modern world from the time of the Restoration of 1868 to the Treaty of Portsmouth of 1905, she viewed with real horror Westernism sweeping in on China like a torrent and threatening entirely to capture it under the name of Democracy. For the isolation which existed under the Tokugawa Shogunate for two and half centuries still lives spiritually in Japan : Japanese national life remains a curious compound of adjustments and half-tones, a rather delicate thing that like a hothouse plant might easily be blasted if left exposed to the cold winds of Reason. To preserve in the second decennium of the twentieth century not only a belief in the divine right of kings, but to propagate officially in every school, in every college, and in every university of the land the cult of the actual divinity of the Emperor, emphatically necessitates a juggling with the problems of the other world of an almost fantastic nature. In the writer's belief the secret of Japanese diplomacy may be traced to this unreal foundation of government, which is further complicated by the haunting conviction

THE OUTLINE OF THE FAR EAST 61

that the Western races are really stronger, more virile, and more efficient than the races of the East, and must infallibly dominate them whenever it comes to an open trial of strength. And if we take this hypothesis as a starting-point obscurity vanishes.

Let us explain. Already after the Russo-Japanese War—i.e. sixteen years ago—all classes of Japanese knew that their material development was wholly insufficient for the fierce competition of the modern world, and that Russia had really been defeated by a miracle. Crushed by taxation to pay the war debt incurred, the Japanese people instinctively favoured a double policy—the exploitation of China for her raw products and the stimulating of Chinese opinion in such a way as to secure, if not the union of the yellow races, at least the general acceptance of the idea that internationally the Far East must be considered as one entity under the hegemony of Japan.

It was when Japanese people were in this mood that the Knox Neutralization scheme of the Manchurian railways was presented to the world (1908) as a solution for the political-territorial tangle which the Russian war had left. That such a proposal, in the circumstances narrated, should have struck the Japanese people much as the Kaiser's telegram to Kruger struck the British people at the time of the South African imbroglio is not at all surprising. It was looked upon as unwarranted interference, almost as an affront. For there was the diplomatic record of the days prior to the Manchurian war to prove that Japan had deliberately and categorically offered to abstain from all interference in Manchuria if Russia would enter into a similar commitment regarding Korea. The fact that the Japanese had been forced to fight a ruinous war, with no real margin of safety either on land or on sea, because that offer had been refused, in their opinion entitled them to a consideration which the jealous Western world was not giving them. It is necessary to insist upon this half-forgotten matter even to the point of weariness, as it is the secret of much tortuous diplomacy. For when the Neutralization scheme fell through, and Japan found the alternative plan for a parallel railway (the Chinchow-Aigun trunkline) being pushed by British and American interests in 1909, she became convinced that a new battle had already commenced having for object her economic restriction on the Asiatic mainland. And although the formal annexation of Korea was successfully accomplished in 1910, in 1911 the British Government insisted on a revision of the Anglo-Japanese Alliance Treaty, inserting a clause which made the inapplicability of that instrument to America absolutely clear.

It was with these things weighing heavily on Japan that the Manchu abdication of February 1912 came—after a British refusal to countenance armed force being lent to retain the dynasty. And when it was plainly shown that Yuan Shih-kai, who for a quarter of a century had been the arch-enemy of the Tokio Government, was being supported by all the Western Powers alike as an instrument to continue the politico-financial policy of the pre-abdication days, every group of Japanese became convinced of the necessity of drastic action.

The outbreak of the World War gave the needed opportunity. Japan consented to declare war on

THE OUTLINE OF THE FAR EAST 63

Germany only on her own conditions. The mishandling of the Tsingtao question by the Allies—the British Government, for instance, could easily have induced Yuan Shih-kai to deliver a twenty-four hours' ultimatum on Germany to evacuate Chinese soil, since the President of China had 50,000 troops almost at Tsingtao's back doors—allowed Japan to make war as if by favour, using the belligerent conditions throughout the world to hasten on a policy which had nothing to do with the issues being so savagely fought out on European soil. And when Yuan Shih-kai, tardily recovering from the surprise into which he had been thrown by the great catastrophe of 1914, declared a war-zone in Shantung province so as to restrict the Japanese military effort, and then cancelled that zone as soon as Tsingtao had been captured, Japanese irritation reached such a point that they were forced to action.

On the 18th January, 1915, they accordingly served their famous Twenty-one Demands on him; and although a violent press defensive did something to mitigate the terms (Group V, which was the outline of a Japanese protectorate, being withdrawn), by means of an ultimatum they forced through all the Manchurian and Shantung articles, with many other valuable closed-door privileges which will be later the cause of international conflict.

Yet even this left Japan dissatisfied: she was still fearful that China would enter the war and thereby regain a certain liberty of action. The direct efforts the Tokio Government made at the end of the year 1915 to prevent such a consummation were followed in 1916 by direct efforts abroad to improve Japan's international standing. It was naturally at Petrograd that Japanese diplomacy first set to work; and as the Bolshevist publication of the Secret Treaties has shown, the Japanese succeeded so well that in 1916 they wrote a reinsurance of their China policy with Russia *aimed at any third Power who might wish to oppose their China schemes.*

But the Russian Revolution totally destroyed the value of this undertaking, whilst almost at the same time China, invited by America to do so, in a most surprising and unexpected way broke off diplomatic relations with Germany, and was on the eve of a formal declaration of war. Seeing the prize once more slipping through their fingers, the Terauchi Ministry developed in the late spring of 1917 a new policy.

Deliberately they associated themselves with the Peiyang military party, promising every kind of financial support if this party would fight under their banner. Nominally acquiescent, the Peiyang party, in spite of the odium cast on them by their Southern adversaries, were still first and last Chinese, i.e. men who knew perfectly well what Japan's plans really were, and who only pretended that they were in entire accord with them. Thus once more there was a play within the play, the number of factors involved being so immense that most people soon lost sight of the main issue—which was that Japan was for the time being merely concentrating on one matter, i.e. pushing Peking to pawn every liquid asset so that Tokio's claims would be so overwhelmingly strong that when it came to a settlement of the Far Eastern question her wishes would be law.

It was under these auspices that Viscount Ishii sailed for the United States, a signal for the keen-witted that things were still deemed unsatisfactory by the Tokio Government and that the last refractory element must be forced into the melting-pot. Finding that two months' sojourn in Washington yielded no tangible results, the Japanese Special Envoy became almost desperate. Then followed a brief and curious departure for New York, with a brief and curious return to Washington, resulting in the Lansing-Ishii Notes of the 2nd November, 1917. That this exchange of notes was very largely prompted by the reports of serious developments of Japanese policy if nothing were done to placate Japanese public opinion, there can to-day be no doubt. The manner in which German emissaries were constantly attempting to enter into relations with Japan—notably at the Scandinavian capitals—is well known to those behind the scenes; and although Japan remained loyal in word and in deed during this dangerous pause in the World War, that temptations of an extraordinary character were dangled before her eyes is an undisputed fact.

And yet even these Notes, with their untenable doctrine of geographical propinquity, did not capture will-o'-the-wisp China. They assisted, no doubt, in the promotion of the peculiar Japanese policy of the year 1918, when so many hundreds of millions of dollars were lent to the Peking Government on ruinous terms to be squandered on a meaningless civil war; but internationally they were failures. England, still the chief Western Power in Eastern Asia, did not recede from the position she took up in her treaty of 1911—that she possessed special interests in China as well as Japan, and that these special interests, British as well as the Japanese special interests, must be maintained. This is a very important fact which has never been given its proper importance : it is a fact which even now troubles Japan.

And then at last Bolshevism, invading Asiatic Russia in the spring of 1918, brought a new complication ; for although there never was any German menace to the Far East as Japanese agents declared, there was certainly a menace to Japanese plans. In the long story of the intrigues and counter-intrigues at Harbin—during the first half of 1918—in which Japan characteristically backed the reactionary General Horvath, master of the Chinese Eastern Railway, in order to gain control of the railway—we see a fire being fanned to a blaze so as to allow deft fingers to secure the chestnuts. Had the reactionary Russian element in the Russian Far East, and among the Cossack communities of Transbaikalia, not been incited to attack the Bolshevists, there would not have been any of the complications which still await solution.

But Japan required frontier warfare, since these activities on the rim of Northern Manchuria allowed her to force through the Sino-Japanese Military Secret Agreement which seemed to bind the Peking Government to her chariot-wheel for a long term of years ; and although the astute use made by the United States of the Czecho-Slovak *impasse* finally brought Allied intervention at Vladivostok and prevented the fruition of the full plan, which was the Japanese military occupation of everything east of Lake Baikal, it is necessary to note that

THE OUTLINE OF THE FAR EAST 67

Japan *has* always acted independently, in spite of the Allies, in Northern Manchuria, in Transbaikalia, and in the Amur province, and is to-day virtual master of Vladivostok and the Russian Far East. The awards made to Japan under the Versailles Treaty, so far from assisting matters in any way, have merely added new and far-reaching complications.

Here we must pause, for the involved outline is now complete. How the imbroglio is to be solved, how a reasonable balance is to be reconstituted for the whole Far East, and peace thereby assured—these things must be separately treated, since they are every whit as complicated as this discussion, which has only touched the fringe of the subject.

CHAPTER III

THE SETTLEMENT OF THE CHINESE QUESTION

THE writer has traced the general outline of the problem as it has appeared to him from an intensive study conducted on the spot ; and although exception may be taken to some of the conclusions he arrived at, it should be carefully noted that these conclusions are to-day the common possession of every unbiassed political student in Eastern Asia who is able to think of the Chinese as normal human beings and who does not deny that they are entitled to international justice.

Two grand facts should emerge from the analysis made : first, that although China has officially and publicly thrown overboard not only her ancient civilization but her system of government, she has not yet succeeded in substituting anything more solid than the theory of Western practice ; secondly, that Japan, following the path of empire that other virile nations have pursued in the past, and believing that the World War has entitled her to a certain local primacy, is pushing deeper and deeper into Continentalism and aspiring more and more openly to the political, commercial, industrial, and military hegemony of Eastern Asia. The question which at once arises is—can these two facts be reconciled ; that is, is it possible for the rebirth of China to be

SETTLEMENT OF THE QUESTION   69

consummated in the face of the imperialistic ambitions of her neighbour? The answer is both yes and no: yes, if the dominant factor in the situation, the maritime Powers, adopt the right policy; no, if instead of enforcing an honest and well-balanced judgment on an admittedly complex and exasperating situation, they follow Pontius Pilate and wash their hands of the whole business.

We have said the maritime Powers—why the maritime Powers?

All the world knows that the British Treaty of Nanking of 1842 and the Perry expedition of 1858 broke up the ancient seclusion of China and Japan and introduced these two countries anew to one another, besides introducing them to Western civilization. But all the world does not know that, dating from this period of seventy years ago, the action of the whole group of maritime Powers, including even the smallest Western nations such as Portugal and Denmark, followed more or less consistent lines under British-American leadership, until the collapse of China in the Korean war destroyed what was sound and creditable in the past record; and by putting the maritime Powers ashore in leased territories and spheres of influence in a vain effort to combat Tsarism and Japanese imperialism, gave policy a wrong twist, and produced general disarray. The conditions which we now face have their origin in events exactly twenty-five years old. They all come by direct descent from the Korean war of 1894–95; and if we are to find a radical and lasting solution for all the perplexing ills of the day it is from the Korean period that the work must commence.

Let it first be understood that the annexation of Korea by Japan in 1910 was an intolerable and unnecessary mistake. The acknowledged protectorate which had existed in that peninsula as a result of the Manchurian war of 1904–05 was all that was necessary to safeguard Japan's strategic interest: anything more than a protectorate inevitably constituted an international danger. For if England requires in Egypt no more than paramountcy to guarantee a vital waterway in her water-empire, certainly Japan has satisfied strategy when she has secured that no hostile forces can seize this hilly promontory which reaches out to within one hundred miles of her coasts. Had that unimaginative statesman Lord Lansdowne really known anything of the history of Asia, he would never have indited his famous dispatch to the Russian Government in 1905, in which he declared that Korea was a region which fell naturally under the sway of Japan—when there was voluminous history since the days of the T'ang dynasty (A.D. 600–900) to prove that Korea fell naturally under the sway of China, and that whenever another Power seized control, it was only to use it as a highway of attack. . . .

The annexation, we say, was an intolerable and unnecessary mistake because of its immediate non-Korean consequences. It made Japan formally and perpetually a Continental Power—that is, gave her an actual stake on the mainland of Asia, a state of affairs which had never previously existed. It committed her to maintaining a large garrison to overawe the Korean population, which was violently hostile. It incited her to extend this land-empire

SETTLEMENT OF THE QUESTION 71

under thinly concealed forms into Southern Manchuria, by giving the railway system which she had captured from Russia a special character, which later she further accentuated by uniting it with the Korean railway system, thus making a Chinese railway and a Japanese railway one and the same entity. It encouraged her to adopt, on the outbreak of the Chinese Revolution and the disappearance of the Manchu dynasty, the doctrine Germany had adopted regarding the Anglo-German understanding of 1900—because Germany had then a secret agreement with Russia—that Manchuria must be held as outside the scope of any agreement regarding China, China meaning China Proper, although this Western geographical distinction is unknown among the Chinese themselves, who for many hundreds of years have treated all Chinese-settled territory precisely on the same footing. Finally, with the outbreak of the World War, it awakened in her the ambition to acquire openly dominant rights northwards to the Amur River, and westwards to the Gobi Desert—the whole original empire of Manchus, which was a Manchu-Mongolian realm governed from Moukden and including by alliance all the banners or "hordes" of Tartary—a thing her military officers declared easy of accomplishment. The complications and irritations which have attended Japanese intervention in the Russian Far East are the natural children of this strange *mésalliance* between an island-empire and the Asiatic mainland; and the almost savage manner in which Japan has tried to seize sole control of the Ussuri Railway and the Chinese Eastern Railway—deliberately wrecking for many months all American attempts under the Stevens Commission to better Russian communications, and starving millions of people in Siberia in consequence, form a sermon on political morality as eloquent as the Sermon on the Mount.

These things have a close and intimate connection with the Chinese question : they are in the nature of the necessary introduction to the settlement. For unless they are closely and intimately associated in the mind as a very large part of the reason why China makes no progress commensurate with her national genius, it is impossible to convey to those who live far distant from these scenes an adequate appreciation of the reality of China's difficulties. The presence of Japan in Korea as lord of the soil; her holding of two fortified areas on the Chinese coast, with their connecting railway systems; her advance into Transbaikalia and inner Mongolia with important military forces, all these things are every whit as paralyzing to Peking as the occupation of Belgium and the Northern French railways by the Germans was paralyzing to Paris; and it is the refusal to recognize that there is absolute analogy in such matters which makes discussion of China's improvement so illusory.

The first and most essential step in the building up of the new Chinese State, if that is really desired, is to have it accepted categorically by all the Powers alike that all railways on Chinese soil are a vital portion of Chinese sovereignty and must be directly controlled by the Chinese Government : that stationmasters, personnel, and police troops must be Chinese citizens, technical foreign help being limited to a set standard; and that all railway concessions

SETTLEMENT OF THE QUESTION 73

within the territory of the Republic *without exception*, from the Amur River in the extreme North to the Red River in the extreme South, must henceforth be considered as Chinese national property, to be handed over as soon as circumstances permit to the National Railway Board.

The test-case is the German Shantung Railway, a system of under five hundred kilometres, very valuable extensions of which Japan has claimed as an inheritance from the original German concessionaires. This state of affairs, if left untouched by International Act, will gradually create a railway *enclave* on the Manchurian model in the heart of old China. For along the course of such railways new railway towns inevitably spring up, bringing all the complications which conflicting jurisdiction creates. To solve this conflict the stronger Power first employs force; then, to give its authority a deeper meaning, it sets up its own courts; administers so-called justice; and sends its police officers far from the zone of the railway to satisfy its judgments. This is already what has happened in Shantung; infallibly it will happen wherever Japanese railways go.

Here, then, is international business of the first importance which cannot be brushed aside. It is absolutely essential that when this test-case comes up again stout defenders be found who will realize that a drama as real to the Chinese people as Kaiserism has been to the European peoples is in process of being enacted; and that beneath the surface every principle for which the war has been fought is at stake—to be honoured or disavowed.

For in the economics of modern communities,

communications have acquired such vast significance that it may be truly said that they constitute to-day the most tangible evidence of sovereignty; and that if they are left in the hands of aliens, surrounded by their own troops, what you have is a *de facto* military occupation, which can be followed only by evacuation or by open annexation. No one with any acquaintance with recent history can deny this elementary proposition; and all arguments that the Chinese administration is unfitted to assume control are placed out of court, seeing that the number of foreign railway experts employed in the Government Railway Service is constantly growing, and that British-constructed railways in China have for a generation been peacefully administered on a system which has never brought the conflict which is inevitable whenever Japanese interests are involved. No matter what attitude is officially adopted by the Powers—no matter how much they may wish to avoid any discussion at all, the Chinese railway issue will be irrevocably forced on the world's attention in the near future, as there are ten thousand miles of delayed railways to be built, and ten thousand troubles will spring from them unless obscurity and obscurantism are forthwith banished.

For lagging not far behind the urgency of this railway matter is the whole question of Chinese trade taxation—a question which has never been more than hastily touched upon and as hastily dropped by foreign negotiators because it has hitherto been beyond their ability and vision to deal with it. Viscount Grey, in a speech which referred to the League of Nations and the good one nation can do another, instanced the Chinese Maritime Customs as

SETTLEMENT OF THE QUESTION 75

an example of successful alien administration, showing by his citation that he was ignorant of the facts. The late Sir Robert Hart, the originator and organizer of this system, which in the popular imagination is supposed to insure the merchant and the manufacturer a successful entry into China, was something of a philosopher and a good deal of a diplomatist; and consequently he was discreet enough not to reveal to the world that he was not doing what he was supposed to be doing. The administration which he erected was simply an accountancy, which was able to justify itself because it was dealing with a foreign thing—the steamer—and which was acclaimed as model and perfect when loans were secured on its receipts, because it made bondholders believe that their interest-coupons were in charge of an institution as solid and as permanent as the Bank of England.

Yet as a matter of fact the Maritime Customs has never touched Chinese life or economics in the slightest, nor has it greatly facilitated trade, which should be its chief function. True, it has enabled merchants to load and unload their cargoes on a water-front against a fixed tariff; but ten minutes beyond that water-front barriers as high as mountains may and do exist—with the markets irrevocably hidden behind them. To those who know that China's foreign trade still only amounts to six silver dollars per annum per head of population (the lowest percentage in the world for the greatest nation of small dealers that has ever existed) the Chinese Maritime Customs is a mere makeshift; a monument to the fierce fight which the maritime nations carried on in the early part of the nineteenth century regarding their inherent right to ports of entry along river and coast; a record of the fact that the Dying God—the Emperor—could not find officers to collect his duties during the great Taiping Rebellion: a proof that the foreign consulates were honest enough to do it for him.

For at the same time that the Maritime Customs came into being as a quasi-foreign creation, the Taiping Rebellion and the loss of great revenues created *likin*, a system of petty levies carried out by means of barriers placed wherever trade passes, which because it accentuates provincialism undoes all the good the Maritime Customs should do with its fixed tariff. Until some Power does for all China what Prussia, in spite of her sins, once did for all Germany—that is, creates a Chinese Zollverein, or Customs Union, making absolute Free Trade within the territories of the Republic a fact—commerce in China will continue to be a medieval enterprise, inviting medieval diplomacy suitable to the courts of petty princes and amounting in the gross to little more than the trade of Switzerland.

Nineteen years ago—to be exact, in 1902—England attempted to be that Power, and in the Mackay Treaty, signed by Lord Inchcape in Shanghai, she agreed to a large tariff increase, abolishing *likin* in the famous Article VIII, on the strict understanding that the treaty was to be inoperative until all the Treaty Powers had signed identical instruments. In 1903, largely because Russia in Manchuria was then such an international peril, America and Japan followed suit—making the same reservations whilst they introduced the same clauses, thus securing that one more pious hope was enshrined

SETTLEMENT OF THE QUESTION 77

in the dust of Chinese archives, to be left there indefinitely like an Egyptian mummy. Since then nothing has been done—nothing for eighteen years; and in the routine decennial tariff revision which took place in Shanghai in 1918, Japan, until the Armistice in Europe of the 11th November, placed every obstacle in the way of China, even acquiring an effective five per cent. levy which has been her treaty right for sixty years.

Now, if the free nations of the world desire that a vastly increased Chinese trade shall assist in wiping out the ill-effects of the European cataclysm which has destroyed the accumulated wealth of half a century, the establishment of a Chinese Zollverein—that is, complete Free Trade within the limits of Chinese territory, with a complete abolition of all provincial and coastwise duties and a complete checking of present abuses—must be secured. At a time when Japanese trade, in spite of a heavy Protectionist tariff, has risen to £500,000,000 a year, or more than £8 per head of population, it is monstrous that Chinese trade should amount to barely £1 per head of population. That the Japanese people on a *per capita* basis should have a commerce eight times larger than the commerce of the Chinese people—born traders, be it remembered—proves conclusively that the whole Chinese fiscal system is radically wrong; and as the commercial nations hold China in thraldom with their commercial treaties, it is they who must make the first move to liberate the purchasing power of the Chinese people. Statisticians are agreed that a legitimate basis of calculation is to assume that China could immediately do a trade per head of population amounting to nearly half the amount of the Japanese trade per person, if all obstructions were cleared away. On this assumption, a China liberated from provincialism and militarism should have an annual turnover of at least 1,200 millions sterling, an amount which would place her in the front rank of trading nations, and (assuming that imports and exports roughly balanced and that the twelve and one-half per cent. Mackay Import Tariff was the average levy) would give her an annual revenue of not far off 100 millions sterling. This sum would provide interest and sinking fund on four times the present amount of the national indebtedness, adding in every loan made for no matter what purpose during the past thirty years, and including all the reckless borrowing of the past quinquennium. It would therefore be easy to secure the service of countless productive loans on such consolidated trade taxation and build up the New China on a solid foundation of sound finance.

If and when this matter of Chinese trade comes up for consideration, another matter which is closely allied to it should not be forgotten.

This is the question of extraterritoriality.

To most people who have lived under their own laws and accepted such a condition as natural all the world over, the idea of extraterritoriality—that is, that in a given territory you are *not* liable to the jurisdiction of the local authority, but come under jurisdiction exercised by officers of your own country—must be surprising.

The origin of extraterritoriality is to be sought on the shores of the Mediterranean, where in the period of transition from the age of Rome's uni-

SETTLEMENT OF THE QUESTION 79

versal empire to that of independent territorial sovereignties, it was held necessary by the maritime cities and republics to appoint officers to take charge of the depositaries of merchandise and exercise jurisdiction over their citizens. This practice, which was well established by the eleventh century, received a great impetus when the Near East fell under the domination of the Mohammedans. The Christian nations, who then entered into relations with the Turkish authority, were careful in their treaties to provide for the establishment of consulates; and the administration of the law of the nation represented was admitted to form an essential part of the consular functions.

It was on this Turkish precedent, then, that practice in the Far East was based. In the first commercial treaty ever entered into between China and a Western Power—the British Treaty of Nanking of 1842—the word extraterritoriality, however, does not occur, and no provision was made for the exercise of jurisdiction by consular officers. In a supplementary treaty for the regulation of trade signed the following year extraterritoriality, however, begins to take shape. It was agreed, for instance, that British merchants and others residing at, or resorting to, the Five Ports opened to trade " shall not go into the surrounding country beyond certain short distances to be named by the local authorities in concert with the British consul and on no pretence for purpose of traffic"; whilst as for seamen and persons belonging to the ships they shall only be allowed to land under special rules. Another clause in the same treaty provides that at each of the five ports opened to trade " one English cruiser will be stationed to enforce good order and discipline amongst the crews of merchant-shipping and to support the necessary authority of the consul over British subjects."

Here extraterritorial jurisdiction emerges, not as it has developed, but as then seemed necessary. It was a police authority over unruly persons of alien race who had forced their way into Chinese anchorages and were so determined to trade that the right to do so had been granted them by the Emperor. All the rough-and-tumble history of the Canton delta during the generation preceding these formal treaties looms up from these clauses: drunken English seamen rowing off from their sailing-ships and indulging in riotous conduct; opium-dealers slipping away in fast boats to hidden creeks where their traffic could be carried on concealed; the Chinese authority, unable to cope with these heavy-fisted men, and only occasionally, when murder or manslaughter was involved, getting hold of the culprit, who was strangled in accordance with the *lex loci*.

Nearly twenty years pass with practice in this inchoate state, the more precise American Treaty of 1844 being generally used as a guide to consular authority. But in the Treaty of Tientsin of 1858 —which was not ratified until Peking had been captured in 1860 and the Son of Heaven had sought safety in flight—Article XVI lays down specifically and absolutely that British subjects guilty of crimes " shall be tried and punished according to the Laws of Great Britain "; and similar clauses being almost immediately inserted in all the treaties with the Powers, extraterritoriality was fully enthroned.

SETTLEMENT OF THE QUESTION

That was exactly sixty years ago, and in sixty years there has been no change save to scatter extraterritorialized persons by the thousand over the length and breadth of the land, often without any consular authority within a week's journey. For the right of residence in the interior, which all missionaries possess by virtue of the French Treaty of Tientsin, and the most-favoured nation clause which is found in all similar instruments, having long ago been annexed not only by countless Japanese but by many other foreigners as well, an entirely new situation exists which urgently calls for reform. Since the Revolution of 1911 and the proclamation of the Republic, China has indeed tacitly accepted this condition of affairs only because she believes that when her case is properly presented no reasonable person will deny that she is entitled to justice.

That is why Young China demands the summary abolition of extraterritoriality, and cries aloud that inasmuch as in the inoperative Shanghai treaties of eighteen years ago it was specifically stated that so soon as a reform of the judicial system was accomplished this foreign jurisdiction would be relinquished, the hour has come for the pledge to be redeemed. For new codes have been adopted under the Republic and a new system of courts; and although there is more theory than practice, the independence of the judiciary forms an integral part of the draft Constitution.

Now, as no questions are so thorny as questions of law and jurisdiction, it is obvious that if this one matter is to be handled successfully it will require a special conference of all the Treaty Powers. The vast and complicated interests which have grown up in China since the Boxer period necessitate a special practice being grafted on to the Chinese administration step by step, rather than any dramatic relinquishment of old rights. It is not possible to refuse to deal with this matter, any more than it is not possible to refuse to deal with the railway question. For since her declaration of war against Germany and Austria, China has had charge of all persons of German and Austrian nationality, in spite of the efforts of the Dutch diplomatic and consular representatives (temporarily in charge of German and Austrian interests) to assume jurisdiction. A number of important Germans and Austrians were long held interned by China in special camps; and that China in the treaties with the enemy Powers has insisted on retaining jurisdiction over citizens of these nations was quite natural. The Chinese police system has made such advances during the past decennium that there can be little doubt that so long as appellate courts, with foreign assessors, are provided for, it should soon be possible to erect a system which will be a half-way house to the total abolition of extraterritoriality.

The precise methods are already matters of dispute, and can certainly not be settled in any casual manner. Some have proposed that there shall be a probationary ten-year period during which China shall be given a trial. Others have declared that the only method is an extension of the mixed court system, although this system in Shanghai is a lamentable failure. Yet another class declare that no modification is possible until conditions throughout the land have been entirely revolutionized. But it is obvious that the complete throwing open of China,

SETTLEMENT OF THE QUESTION 83

with the universal right of trade and residence freely conceded, cannot be satisfactorily arranged if a favoured class is removed from police control—particularly such men as Japanese peddlers, who in hundreds and thousands roam the land retailing great and increasing quantities of morphia and opium in defiance of the law of the land.

The solution which the writer has already brought to the notice of Parliament and of Chambers of Commerce in England is the creation of trading zones ten miles wide along all lines of communication.

If the old model which was originated by Tsarist Russia when she built the Manchuria Railways a quarter of a century ago is adopted without the bad features, such zones can speedily make all railways and rivers throughout the country symbols of the New China. For, providing all necessary police and taxing powers are retained by the Chinese State (without judicial rights), it will be possible to banish all restrictions regarding foreign residence and factories and warehouses, and thus to cover the land, wherever trade and produce flow, with a chain of Euro-Chinese interests. The effects of such a development would be economically incalculable. Within a brief period the treaty port would become a mere port of entry, industrial interests concentrating near their raw materials and becoming at once a pledge and a guarantee of the new order. Factories which are now merely counted by dozens would rise in hundreds and thousands. The presence of foreign interests and foreign residents along all lines of communications would secure in the matter of abolition of internal trade taxation in return for increased maritime customs duties, that no abuses by local officials grew up. In the opinion of the writer the solution of a very knotty problem is contained in this formula.

In this discussion we have travelled the whole road which it is possible to travel in one stage. To proceed further would entangle issues in the minds of those who are anxious to understand. Chinese currency, the Chinese debt, the Chinese civil and military administration, and the question of parliamentary government, are best considered separately as the problem of Peking. They belong to a different category from the semi-foreign issues already discussed, because they are of a different ancestry.

CHAPTER IV

THE PROBLEM OF PEKING

THE problem of Peking is so peculiar that no parallel case exists in any other part of the world. Turkey is sometimes quoted as a similar instance; but the differences between China and Turkey are greater than the points of resemblance. Turkey comprises a mixture of races; the Chinese are absolutely homogeneous. The rule of the Ottoman Turks was based on military conquest; the Manchus, who were their prototypes, were summarily ousted ten years ago, and for many a day prior to their actual collapse had not much more power than the errant descendants of Genghiz Khan. Then Turkey is so close to Europe that her problem is an European issue; China is so far distant that she is remote even to India. Turkey pretended to reform, and then surrendered to the Young Turks, who were virtually Young Germans. The Tu-chün, or military governors in China and their henchmen, may perhaps be held the equivalent of this truculent breed; yet even these semi-ignorant leaders pay homage to the literary traditions of the race, worship formality, and declare that they represent a transitional stage which will soon give way to a new brotherhood.

For the time being, however, what we have to-day, pending the settlement, is rule by velleities—i.e. by volition in its lowest form, which only takes on a positive character when a direct assault is made on the *lares* and *penates* of the office-holders. In the past it has been clearly shown how every time the defenders of the Republic have attempted to adopt definite formulæ in place of this obscurantism, they have been beaten into retirement in the provinces because they have lacked the necessary force to win. With this inchoate condition in the capital and with the chief cities held by military rule, watchful drifting has become the avowed policy. And although all Chinese know perfectly well that without organization, and without the supremacy of the civil authority, it is vain to hope for national solidarity or greatness, no single man has yet been able to effect any lasting improvement. Thus, although the empire has gone never to return, and although a definite and recognizable advance in ideas is generally admitted to have occurred throughout China, obscure causes which must be referred back to climate and soil, and to the city type, which a hundred city-bred generations have evolved, tend to perpetuate this political palsy and to make many foreign critics declare there is actual chaos and retrogression. That behind all this—deep buried in the twilight of a myriad homes—the supreme explanation is to be sought in the very mild impulses of the race, which are expressed in the quietist doctrines animating Chinese society, is the writer's profound conviction. And so does it happen that the Chinese people have come to think that they have been caught in the Caudine Forks, and that it is the Japanese who are striving mightily to play the part of the Samnites and make them pass under the yoke.

II

What are the vital difficulties at the present moment in the way of civil authority being so constituted as to be effective ?

First, and greatest of all, there is the question of Parliament and the rôle it should play in the life of the State. Round this question a fierce struggle has raged from the very inception of the Republic, because the abdication of the Manchus was only secured by a compromise so framed that Conservatives and Radicals could interpret that dramatic act much as they pleased. According to Article 53 of the Nanking provisional Constitution, promulgated in January 1912, and accepted as the law of the land, within ten months of that date a National Assembly was to be convened, to frame the permanent Constitution and to be the articulate voice of the nation. The first full Parliament should therefore have assembled in Peking by October 1912; it did not meet until April 1913, owing to deliberate obstruction in the elections practised by Yuan Shih-kai—the last act of which was the assassination of the Southern leader Sung Chiao-jen, who was admittedly the hope of the genuinely Republican party. This Parliament was not yet fully organized when Yuan Shih-kai, alleging that the National Council (sitting prior to the convocation of Parliament) had given him power to do so, forced through the great Reorganization Loan over Parliament's head, denying that it had the right to scrutinize this important measure, and being supported in his unconstitutional and reactionary policy by five Powers—England, France, Germany, Russia, and Japan. Native arms and foreign diplomacy thus formed an unholy alliance in China in 1913.

This first great assault on the Republic was followed by a six-month period of intimidation and bribery, after which Yuan Shih-kai finally secured the passage of the Presidential Election Law and was elected full president for the first five-year term. Thereupon, having a complete legal title, he carried out his *coup d'état* of the 4th November, 1913, and unseated all Southern members of Parliament, following this by destroying by means of bogus enactments the legal framework on which international recognition of the Republic had been accorded; finally capping it all two years later by an elaborate ballot-fraud whereby he declared himself elected Emperor of the Chinese *à la* Napoleon and head of a so-called Constitutional Monarchy. That comprises the complete story of the first four years of the rule of Peking over the provinces under the Republic and shows what a hollow mockery it was.

With Yuan Shih-kai's death in June 1916, the 1913 Parliament returned to the capital—weakened but still determined to consummate its main work, which was the formal passage of a permanent Constitution, the draft of which had been so long complete. In spite of every kind of opposition, such progress was made that in less than a year, with the exception of the seven clauses which follow, the two Houses had passed the completed instrument through its second reading, and would have entirely terminated the work had there not been deliberate military obstruction. The seven disputed clauses were :—

Article 32. The ordinary sessions of the National Assembly shall begin on the 1st August of each year.

Article 35. Both Houses shall meet in joint session at the opening and closing of the National Assembly. If one House suspends its session, the other House shall do likewise during the same period. When the House of Representatives is dissolved, the Senate shall adjourn during the same period.

Article 75. With the concurrence of two-thirds or more of the members of the Senate present, the President may dissolve the House of Representatives, but there must not be a second dissolution during the period of the same session.

When the House of Representatives is dissolved by the President another election shall take place immediately, and the convocation of the House at a fixed date within five months should be effected to continue the session.

Article 82. When a vote of want of confidence in the Cabinet Ministers is passed, if the President does not dissolve the House of Representatives according to the provisions made in Article 75, he should remove the Cabinet Ministers.

Article 92. Should the President disapprove of any bill of law passed by the National Assembly, he shall, within the period allowed for promulgation, state the reason of his disapproval and request the reconsideration of the same by the National Assembly. If a bill has not been submitted with a request for reconsideration and the period of promulgation has passed, it shall become law. But the above shall not apply to the case when the session of the National Assembly is adjourned or the House of Representatives dissolved before the period for the promulgation is ended

Article 107. The method of organization of the Auditing Department and the qualifications of auditors shall be fixed by law. During his term of office the auditor shall not be dismissed or transferred to any other duty or his salary reduced except in accordance with the law. The manner of punishment of auditors shall be fixed by law.

Article 108. The Chief of the Auditing Department shall be elected by the Senate. The Chief of the Auditing Department may attend sittings of both Houses and report on the audit with explanatory statements.

Now, even to those who are not over-familiar with constitutional enactments the aim and purpose of these Articles should be tolerably clear: they were drafted to secure the real independence and supremacy of the National Assembly and to serve as checks against abuses which experience had shown were the chief dangers.

Article 82 had a certain technical importance owing to the 1918 Presidential election, which was a highly contentious matter. Articles 85 and 75, placing the Senate in a very strong constitutional position *vis-à-vis* the Chief Executive, and restricting his power over the Lower House, were looked upon by the militarist party as their death-warrant; whilst Article 82, which strictly defines the President's action when a vote of want of confidence in the Cabinet Ministers is passed, contains the very essence of the whole constitutional fight. Article 92 dealing with the President's suspensive veto has been looked upon as hardly less important, and the two concluding Articles, in which Audit is so strictly defined and the control over the National Purse retained by this method after supplies have been actually voted, has been one of the bitterest subjects of dispute. Finally, just before the rupture, a proposal to tack on to the Constitution an additional chapter on local government, dealing with the governing of the provinces, had taken such concrete form that a complete draft had been made; and as in this draft the powers given to Provincial Assemblies were very large, the sweeping away of the Tuchün system was imminent.

THE PROBLEM OF PEKING 91

In June 1917, although the question of an immediate declaration of war against Germany and Austria was the technical reason, this parliamentary question brought the expected crisis. For the second time in the brief life of the Republic the party with whom power really rested—the military element—saw its existence openly menaced. Accordingly, after a long and bitter struggle behind the scenes, President Li Yuan-hung was finally intimidated into promulgating a Mandate of Dissolution, although he had no constitutional right to do so ; and as the capital was already under the control of the military, Parliament was forced to scatter.

No doubt it was the fact that the immediate sequel to this dissolution was a burlesque restoration of the Manchus, lasting eleven days, which confused the Northern military party. Had they been well advised, they would have hastened the summoning of a new Parliament on the valid election law of 1918, as has now been done, and sought an immediate compromise on the seven Articles. But finding the field absolutely free—after they had thrown down the Manchus again—and being fearful of the future, they summoned a packed and illegal National Council, under the so-called authority of the provisional Constitution ; instructed this body to alter the election law, and then held a general election, which sent to Peking two greatly reduced, packed Houses in time to carry out the quinquennial Presidential election. Their official candidate, curiously enough, was probably the best man in China, Hsü Shih-chang, a former viceroy of Manchuria, who by training and natural inclination is sufficiently broad-minded to settle the problem—if supported.

His tenure of office has already brought improvement, in that the entire body of official opinion now acquiesces in the view that the elimination of the army as a political factor must be accomplished to have any solidarity at all; but this has not yet healed the breach with South China or made Canton willing to discuss the federal plan which all Moderates now favour. Peking is, therefore, still denounced, somewhat unfairly, since it is in favour of a compromise which will give provincial Home Rule.

III

Now, it must be plain from this account that something has been radically wrong with foreign diplomacy as well as with Chinese hearts for such a record to stand to the discredit of Peking. The type of diplomatic agent the several Allied governments have maintained in the Chinese capital during the Republican period has not been the type which the conditions emphatically call for. With the exception of the United States, all the Allied representatives since the inception of the Republic have been men lamentably untrained in the part played in the governing of their own countries by their own Legislatures. Had this not been so, no such stupidity would have been shown as in 1913, when with a golden opportunity to enforce constitutionalism on the leader of the militarists—Yuan Shih-kai—by demanding Parliamentary ratification of a prime financial measure, and thus securing once and for all that financial centralization in China was based on legislative acts, foreign ministers deliberately

THE PROBLEM OF PEKING

assisted the Dictator to make a *coup d'état* by means of foreign money, and thus gave the quarrel a vicious international character. The day has surely passed when such things can be tolerated; but until England, France, Italy, and Japan publicly repent, and send as envoys to the Chinese capital men specially selected by virtue of a long parliamentary experience in their own countries—plenipotentiaries who thoroughly understand the necessity of the supremacy of the Legislature even in China —there will be no great improvement in Peking. For China to-day leans absolutely and entirely on the West—no matter what else may be pretended; and instead of rebuffing the widespread desire to benefit by the superior political knowledge of Europe and America, that desire should be stimulated in every possible way, and the fact made perfectly clear by the acts of the accredited foreign representatives that a strong government, based on constitutionalism, is their one and only concern.

This viewpoint is fortified when we consider the actual nature of the contact between the foreign legations and the metropolitan government. That contact is not diplomatic in the ordinary sense of the word : rather is it financial and economic, having come by direct descent from the time when the first foreign representatives in the Canton factory days were Superintendents of Trade. The foreign ministers are therefore principally concerned with questions arising out of loan contracts ; with questions concerning the periodic release of surpluses of revenue collections which have been almost entirely hypothecated abroad ; with disputes arising from the interpretation of treaties and covenants governing commerce and residence and land-ownership—in a word, all the *disjecta membra* of a mercantile imperialism. And because of this peculiar heredity—with ninety years of strife and gunboat methods behind it—Peking diplomacy, encased since 1900 in a fortified diplomatic quarter, has developed a peculiar mentality among those who interpret it, making them small, irritable, and meticulous when imagination and common sense and personal acquaintance with the liberating world-movement of the day are emphatically required.

These matters—and what they directly signify—are of the highest importance. For the two ministries on which China's future largely depends, because they are the interpreters of the civilization and organization which the breakdown of the Confucian state-system has brought into the country, are simply the Ministry of Finance and the Ministry of Communications. Virtually, all the politico-financial business arising out of foreign intercourse is in their hands, and only indirectly in the hands of the Chinese Foreign Office. Long ago it should have been the aim of all the liberal Powers to place under the roof of these two Boards—fully centralized and fully defined—all matters which are justly the objects of their official concern. Publication of facts and figures should have been substituted for haggling about details—not hypothecation or alien control, but organization should have been the goal. The Ministry of Finance, with its many foreign Bond Issues, should not only have direct and absolute control over the great sources of revenue, but should have been stimulated into

THE PROBLEM OF PEKING

issuing proper quarterly statements in Chinese and English, thus bringing light into dark places. There should not have been a constant policy of frightening the Chinese people with visions of a Foreign Debt Bureau under foreign control on the Egyptian-Turkish model. A real Chinese service of the national debt, in place of the present semi-foreign pawn-broking methods; a proper currency system, with token coins and bank-notes maintained at parity—these things would be far more beneficial to the world at large than spheres of influence, or personal victories signalized by the appointment of favoured nationals to sinecures. At present all these questions are inextricably and hopelessly confused; but inasmuch as the five-year suspension of the Boxer indemnities will afford an opportunity before there is any resumption of the payments for a wholesale review of the financial problem, this view of reform must be vindicated.

For depending directly on revenue-control and currency is the whole question of the credit of the Chinese people. China has virtually accepted as her money standard the silver dollar of the same weight and fineness as the Mexican dollar, and the people are becoming accustomed to it. Many hundred million of these units have been actually coined by the Chinese mints, not to speak of the hundreds of millions imported in the past from Mexico and melted in part into sycee. But this currency is officially still only a shopping currency; the money of account is still the tael, which pass from one emporium to another and finally into the creditor-banks in standardized lumps of bullion which vary according to locality.

From the international point of view this matter of the currency, and the whole loan policy of the Powers, is indeed in as pretty a diplomatic tangle as a Talleyrand could desire. Nearly twelve years ago, on American initiative, a currency loan of 50 million gold dollars was signed; but the Revolution of 1911 prevented either the loan being floated or any true reorganization being attempted. Four Powers participated in this loan, England, America, France, and Germany, this official group being later expanded by the admission of Russia and Japan, who had protested that they were being discriminated against by being excluded. Meanwhile in 1913 America dropped out of participation in Chinese finance because of President Wilson's well-known declaration that the conditions of foreign loans in China seemed to touch very nearly the administrative independence of the Chinese people, transactions of this character being obnoxious to the principles upon which the American Government rested. This reduced the number of participating countries to five. Since the World War Germany has, of course, had her partnership in the official Consortium cancelled; and the bankruptcy of Russia likewise precludes her from being a sponsor of any Chinese loan.

The virtual destruction of the old Consortium led the United States in 1919 to secure the adhesion of the three most interested Powers, England, Japan and France, to a new formula. Concentrating on the most essential aspect of Chinese reconstruction—the building of new railways—the United States propounded the doctrine that all building contracts which had not been proceeded with

THE PROBLEM OF PEKING

should be pooled, and the Consortium as a unified financial board take them over. After Japanese objections regarding South Manchuria had been partly met by allocating to her exclusively the building of all lines that could be looked upon as feeders of the South Manchuria system, the Consortium announced that it had achieved complete agreement, and that it was prepared to lend money to the Peking Government on certain terms. These terms have never been officially disclosed—at least not fully—but in regard to railways, for which several hundred millions sterling are required, it is believed that a general control over all Chinese railways is desired—something which no Chinese Government worthy of the name can concede, since the railways are to be " detached " from the general administration and the Japanese monopoly in Manchuria virtually recognized. Moreover, it is gravely to be doubted whether any system of enormous gold loans in a silver-standard country which is gradually installing a modern credit system would not do more harm than good.

The following should make this clear. The loans, being gold loans, are paid over to China in silver credits at exchange rates, which are " worked " by the banks in an admittedly scandalous manner. In the case of the £25,000,000 sterling Reorganization Loan of 1913, it was dicovered by chance that the instalments paid over in Peking were placed to China's credit at a profit of 3 per cent. to the participant banks over and above legitimate commission and over and above the true market rates. Similarly, by various intricate juggling methods, nominally made in the interests of the foreign bondholders, instalments for the service of foreign loans must be paid monthly into the foreign issuing banks, who allow the Chinese Government 2 per cent. annual interest, and thus make privately at least 5 per cent. per annum from the use of the Chinese Government's moneys. Furthermore, other abuses have grown up. Thus in 1915, nominally to safeguard the interest of the bondholders and in defiance of the particular loan agreement involved, the foreign banks stopped payment to China of 10 million dollars of salt surplus, and for four years held this amount in their coffers as a "reserve" to pay Chinese coupons, allowing China 2 per cent. per annum on this amount and making at least 5 per cent. net profit per annum on the transaction. The issuing banks have therefore been placed by their governments in the immoral position of being able to utilize China's financial resources in their own interests under the plea that they are safeguarding the interests of the bondholders. That this abuse, which has largely arisen because of the presence in Peking of diplomatic representatives who know little or nothing of the money market, must be terminated at an early date cannot be refuted.

Fortunately, China has at last been able to do something herself of an eminently practical nature. In 1920 began the organization of a Chinese Bankers Association, under the leadership of the two Government banks, the Bank of China and the Bank of Communications, a clear reply to the foreign Consortium. By 1921 upwards of thirty modern Chinese banks had adhered to this organization, and several silver loans for productive purposes

THE PROBLEM OF PEKING

made to the Government. One for about a million sterling provided funds for making good the shortage in rolling-stock on the Government railways. A second made provision for the erection of the Central Mint at Shanghai where the free coinage of standard Republican dollars will commence from some date in 1922. Thus the Chinese have gone a long way towards solving by themselves the thorny currency problem and the question of providing funds for their national development.

For there is no doubt that Chinese credit should be used as far as possible for the flotation of silver internal loans in priority to foreign gold loans. It is better for the Chinese people to borrow at 12 per cent. internally than at 8 per cent. or 9 per cent. externally. The whole history of war finance shows that the foreign loan is the enemy, and that borrowing at home is the basis of sound business. Doubly so is this the case in silver-using countries where gold commitments play havoc with the national balanc sheet.

It is therefore imperative that there should be a modification of the foreign Consortium, and a new agreement made which will empower Member Bankers to participate in silver loans on terms to be arranged with the Chinese Bankers Association. China must be given a free hand in all financial operations carried out within the limits of Chinese territory. To this view the principal British banks in China are already inclined to assent. It is a remarkable fact that since the Armistice Chinese mercantile interests have shown sounder and more up-to-date methods than foreign nations.

IV

The extraordinary nature of the railway tangle to-day is due both to the false principles on which the development of Chinese railways has been conducted in the past, and to the hopes still cherished by some Powers, notably Japan, that the control of Chinese communications is a stepping-stone to political domination.

We have already sufficiently insisted upon the nationalization of Chinese railways—that is, on the necessity of all railways being unified in a common system, and so-called railway concessions being handed over to the Ministry of Communications as soon as construction work is completed. In the past the method pursued by foreign interests has been as follows. After a bitter struggle in the dark, with every rival Legation working through every possible agency to prevent consummation, a railway concession (i.e. a building concession) is granted to a single concessionaire or to a group of concessionaires, which provides for the issue of a gold loan on the security of the given line the amortization of that loan after a certain period, and the appointment of a chief engineer and a chief accountant of the concessionaire's nationality—the whole enterprise being nominally controlled by a Chinese director-general. The granting of this concession, however, is held to carry certain rights, irrespective of the real interests of the country; for instance, the concessionaire considers it necessary to stop the building of any line in his vicinity, particularly parallel lines, and sometimes feeder lines if contracted for by other parties. Moreover, the sphere of influence is still such a cherished doctrine among the diplomatic fraternity, that the invasion of a given sphere by a contractor of rival nationality is one of the most dangerous crimes, providing a local *casus belli* which is fought out bitterly in the *coulisses* of the various ministries and throughout the Far Eastern press. Asia Minor could hardly provide a more brilliantly tinted map than the present railway map of China when it is coloured according to the nationality of each concessionaire group. There is consequently not complete unity in Chinese railways, either in administration or in finance; and whilst nominally the Ministry of Communications is in supreme command, in practice a centralized government control, of the type which the war has made a commonplace, is still unrealizable.

It is this centralized control which must be brought to China—with every railway on Chinese soil directly controlled from Peking. The fact that existing lines are already large dividend-earners should simplify the solution of the problem—which, as in the case of currency, should be worked out by government experts in the employ of China, who will not be in any way influenced by the old-fashioned mercantile imperialism. So far as railway statistics and returns are concerned, China for some years has possessed a most modern system.

But China requires a complete reform for internal political reasons as well as for external. For, as in the case of every other modern convenience, control cannot be properly centralized unless the abuses which are rapidly becoming stereotyped are absolutely checked. It is imperative to lay down and accept the same principles as have proved beneficial in other countries. For that reason the railway proposals of the foreign Consortium must be modified and no attempt to build up an un-Chinese system officially supported. China contains nearly all the capital necessary for her railways: foreign co-operation can expedite the tapping of this wealth.

The urgent matter of a system of national, hard-surface highways should not be lost sight of. Republican China has inherited from the Manchus a great system of Imperial highways, useless for modern purposes since they are unmetalled, but covering a great portion of the land and capable of knitting the country very closely together, besides vastly increasing the prestige of Peking. The allocation of a portion of the surplus from increased Customs duties to national road-building would in a decade work miracles of education among the people and strengthen the voice of authority. With credit and currency restored, and with a network of railways and roads covering the twenty-two provinces, republican China might soon become as important a factor in world commerce and world industry as the United States, since the supply of men and women is virtually endless, and is now increasing at the rate of several million persons a year. Only by liberating the natural money-making genius of the Chinese people and by giving them reasonable economic guarantees can Western civilization justify its invasion of Cathay and its remorseless destruction of the old gods.

THE PROBLEM OF PEKING

V

There remains one question, and one only, to discuss.

This is the policing of the country.

The Chinese army, as has been clearly shown, has degenerated into a political pawn. To transfer it back to its proper sphere, and to reduce its numbers, is' the work of education and sympathy as well as of political compromise. For it must be remembered that what the provincial generals have been doing in regard to the provincial capitals and along the connecting railways has been largely taught them by what they see in the metropolis and along the railway leading from the sea to Peking. Foreign garrisons, placed in the capital and at each strategic point in the metropolitan province under the Boxer protocol, have for twenty years accustomed men to the belief that soldiers are an essential part of politics—national as well as international—and that it is only the man with the rifle who is the man with a policy. In the opinion of the writer justice as well as expediency requires a relaxation of the safeguards established as a result of the now forgotten siege of the Legations. The few thousand foreign troops in North China no longer mean what they once did; the Chinese army is to-day far too powerful in artillery to be overawed by what was once an impressive force. To protract what is a daily source of irritation is a senseless policy: no statesman can endorse it.

A foreign evacuation protocol is therefore just as essential as an evacuation by Chinese generals of the provincial capitals: the two things should go hand in hand. There is no need for haste; but the drafting of a definite scheme of dates to cover evacuation stage by stage is to-day essential. In this scheme it is essential that all troops belonging to one province shall not be allowed to occupy the territory of another province, but must be evacuated home.

Already there is an efficient gendarmerie in Peking, perfectly trustworthy and perfectly able to do its duty if police and politics are separated. The Peking police schools are gradually transferring more and more men to various parts of the country; and that recruits are excellent and well-trained is shown by the fact that the foreign municipality of Shanghai is requisitioning them and finding them superior to Japanese constables. A sufficient number is all that is required—half a million for the whole country would guarantee peace and security and largely banish the present unrest.

If we are to ensure a happy morrow for the Chinese, all the things which we have touched upon must be considered as one organic whole—to be handled with idealism and practical common sense. The problem of Peking should be made the problem of Europe and America, it should be treated as an intimate and not as an insoluble matter, since it has directly grown out of the superior strength in peace and war of the Western man, and urgently demands not his indifference but his sympathy and help.

CHAPTER V

IF JAPAN REFUSES?

WE have reached the last phase—the question of Japan.

Until Japan defeated China in 1894, the condition of her armaments, her finance, and her industry was of a modest and even primitive nature. She had an army of a hundred thousand soldiers; a navy comprising a few protected cruisers; a silver currency mixed with the remains of an abortive National Bank system copied (on the late Prince Ito's recommendation) from America; and a foreign trade of a hundred million dollars a year. By her Treaty of Peace, however, she received forty million pounds in sterling; established a gold exchange standard, which was maintained by keeping in London her main stock of the yellow metal (a practice partially continued even to-day, which has a profound and little understood effect on Far Eastern politics); and almost immediately recovered from Western nations her passionately contested tariff and the judicial autonomy (the new treaties becoming operative in 1899).

It is from this date, then, that Japan definitely enters international politics; the rock on which she built was defeated China. Prior to that she had barely been more than a third-class Power, with little vision of greater days. Troubled by many internal problems, her efforts to cope with the reorganization of her finances had signally failed. It is true that the matter of her inconvertible paper money had been solved, and a Central Bank of Issue, modelled on the Belgian National Bank, established before Chinese wealth had been tapped. But without the stock of gold won by the Chinese war it is difficult to believe that her exchange standard, which is the head and front of her banking and industrial system, could have been created. In this, as in other matters, Japan's prototype—absolutely and entirely—was Germany of the *post* 1870-71 period. Germany was her light and her guide, and almost every step that Prussia took after her defeat of France was sedulously copied.

Although she emerged from her Chinese war financially satisfied, Japan was in many ways greatly embittered. Her original Treaty of Peace, which had included the cession of the Liaotung peninsula, had been torn up by the action of Russia, Germany, and France, who had interposed a blunt fiat backed by battleships; and she had been forced to return to China what she had already annexed. She was bitterly hurt by this—both on account of the international humiliation, and because her real motives had been misunderstood. She had believed that the only method of terminating Manchu intrigue in the Korean peninsula was completely to cut off all land-contact between the Courts of Peking and Seoul; the Liaotung was therefore desired not so much as a Japanese colony as a buffer-territory between two capitals united by historic ties, and by a thousand-mile Imperial highway along which Korea's tribute missions had journeyed for so many

IF JAPAN REFUSES? 107

centuries. Obsessed with this point of view, which was totally unrelated to world-politics, the shock to her pride was very great when she was peremptorily shown that the Yellow Sea was not a lake, but part of a general scheme of things which she must envisage as a whole, with her eyes specially fixed on the heavy guns of the ships from the West.

The action of England had been different from the action of the three Continental Powers. England had declined to be associated with the intervention, although during the period of the war she had frankly warned Japan off all China treaty ports, declaring that she would not tolerate interference with her trade. Nevertheless England was so friendly that it was largely due to her initiative that tariff and judicial subjection were so rapidly abolished, even America not caring to deal with the matter until Britain had spoken.

By 1895, therefore, Japan had certain very clear-cut ideas on international politics. She had been given practical proofs of hostility and of qualified friendship, and American silence during this critical period had told her that the United States as a world-Power was still more of a theory than a fact. Japan was still so weak that she did not dare to challenge what almost immediately took place in Korea because the buffer-territory idea had been destroyed; and the fearful assassination of the old Korean Queen by *Soshi* and secret agents of the Japanese Legation showed how desperate the collapse of her plans had made her. Russian influence now not only took the place of Chinese influence in Korea, but by her railway plans the great Northern Power showed that her goal was the ice-free waters of the Yellow Sea, which she desired to dominate. The curious and perverse after-war diplomacy of Li Hung Chang, which began with secret conversations at the Tsar's coronation in Moscow in 1896, and finally culminated in acquiescence in the cool Slav seizure of Port Arthur, were daggers in the heart of Japan—which she was unable to ward off. But in 1900, on the occasion of the Boxer explosion, by winning the esteem of the world by the excellence of her expeditionary force, she prepared the ground for what subsequently happened. The Colossus of the North, after playing for more than half a century like a cat with a mouse with Chinese sovereignty, had become too bold. Casting off the fiction of friendly co-operation, which had been her insistent cry ever since Muravieff had first sailed down the Amur in the middle of the nineteenth century, Russia had invaded all Manchuria and established garrisons even to the mouth of the Yalu, her intrigues in Seoul to obtain the lease of a harbour at the toe of the Korean boot—Masampo for choice—being so insistent as to make the Mikado's country seethe with rage.

In 1904 Japan hazarded the impossible. The splendid gesture which involved her in war with Russia was forced on her; it was in every sense a war which had to be fought if Japan were to retain her real independence. There is no question but that Russia directly and categorically refused all real accommodation; she bluffed and hoped against hope to the very end. Japan fought desperately and won a qualified victory which would have been much more justly settled had it not been for the impetuosity of the late President Roosevelt. The

IF JAPAN REFUSES? 109

Treaty of Peace, which would have been signed in Peking and not at Portsmouth, had all the surrounding circumstances been properly understood, was an unfortunate instrument; like the Lansing-Ishii Notes, it was a monument of haste rather than of prescience. A wiser policy would have regarded the Scriptural invocation regarding peacemakers as politically unsuitable to the circumstances and left the protagonists strictly alone. Had that been done both would have come to their senses, and all history might have been different in the West as in the East; for both were not more than four or five months off complete exhaustion. Empty ammunition-wagons, depleted battalions, and ominous murmurs from the civil population—these are the only things that bureaucratic governments appreciate. Neither Russia nor Japan could have faced in 1905 another winter campaign.

II

We have said the Treaty of Peace should have been signed in Peking : had that been done it would not have been necessary to have had a double arrangement—one between Japan and Russia, followed by a separate ratification between China and Japan. Too little attention has been directed to the action Japan took in December 1905 in the Chinese capital: all the essential business—the business really worth recording as a result of the territorial struggle, since it involved the lord of the soil—took place here. Briefly, it was in this month of December 1905—sixteen years ago—that Japan first clearly showed political immorality. From the practical point of view, all that the Portsmouth Treaty had done, with the exception of recognizing the old Japanese claim to half of Saghalien, was to record an accomplished fact—namely, Russia's international humiliation because of the crass failure of her army and navy. The curious connection of China with the imbroglio, arising from the circumstance that the entire war had been waged on her soil, and was directly concerned with certain grants she had been induced to make in the matter of a harbour, two railways, and the Yalu forest concession—this curious connection was never rightfully considered, and China was treated as negligible. Manchuria being as Chinese as the metropolitan province of Chihli, a proper and decent neighbourly spirit, not to speak of expediency and foresight, should have prompted Japan to insist on the war settlement being a tripartite agreement to which three contracting parties —Russia, China, and Japan—put their signatures, thus doing away entirely with the past causes of friction. But this would have meant the banishment of obscurantism; and Japan abroad thrives on organized opposition to inquiry and reform as on nothing else. To put it squarely, Japan in 1905, had she been honest, should have demanded that the whole Manchurian railway enterprise be retroceded to China—the trans-Manchurian lines as well as the South Manchurian—and then converted into a standard-gauge railway, after a lapse of time just sufficient to allow Russia to build the Amur railway and link up her Far Eastern possessions on her own territory. Had Japan taken this one step she would have made China her ally for all time, trebled her

IF JAPAN REFUSES?   111

influence in every part of her neighbour's vast territories, and so handicapped Westernism that it is extremely doubtful whether any further development of European or American influence or industrial enterprise would have been possible. There is also little doubt that in such circumstances the Manchu dynasty would never have fallen as it did in 1912, but would have been converted very peacefully into a constitutional monarchy. Humiliation in foreign affairs was· the last straw to break the camel's back, and in this humiliation Japan played the largest part. The short-sightedness of Japanese policy, therefore, has been the ally of republicanism in the Far East, the sponsor of Western influence, and the enemy of the peace and dignity of the Japanese Imperial House, which is to-day swaying ominously under the high winds of democratic revolt, and may yet encounter a terrible end.

III

The treaty which Japan signed with China, December 1905, actually consisted of the two following clauses only; that it should have been so brief shows the spirit in which Japan negotiated. The clauses read :—

Article I

The Imperial Chinese Government consent to all the transfers and assignments made by Russia to Japan by Articles V and VI of the Treaty of Peace above mentioned

Article II

The Imperial Japanese Government engage that in regard to the leased territory, as well as in matters of railway construction and exploitation, they will as far as circumstances permit conform to the original agreements concluded between China and Russia. In case any question arises in the future on these subjects the Japanese Government will decide it in consultation with the Chinese Government.

Why this brevity? For very peculiar and indeed Machiavellian reasons.

No matter what the spirit of Tsarist Russia may have been in the long struggle to reach "warm water," it is fact that every instrument the Northern Power wrote with the Peking Government from 1896 to her disastrous war with Japan at least carefully preserved the fiction that enterprises on Chinese soil were held in *usufruct*: Russia had the use and profit, but not the property. This is of the highest importance. It was specifically provided, for instance, in the Port Arthur lease (Article VI), that "Port Arthur shall be a naval port for the sole use of Russian and Chinese men-of-war," i.e. it was an anchorage to which China had as much right as Russia. When in 1905 this matter was brought up in the Sino-Japanese negotiations, the Japanese plenipotentiaries immediately took exception to the contention, and declared that it was on record that on the only occasion during the period of the Russian lease that two Chinese cruisers had attempted to dock, the Russians had denied the right, and therefore the right had lapsed. China was in a position to prove from the logbooks of the two cruisers in question that the Russian harbour authorities had signalled on the occasion in question " docks occupied : no accommodation," and the Japanese negotiators, finally convinced that the point was against them, acted in a manner which sheds an interesting

IF JAPAN REFUSES ? 113

light on their constant professions of friendship for " a kindred Asiatic race." The naval authorities were at once given orders to strip the Port Arthur docks completely and entirely so that there should be no dockyard facilities left; and Port Arthur, which had sheltered a Russian fleet more formidable than the entire Japanese navy in 1904, was made a derelict and rated as a second-class naval station to keep the Chinese out and allow Japan gradually to assume the right of eminent domain. These are the things as they really occur in the Far East—these are the foreign policies of Japan unmasked.

In addition to the treaty we have quoted, Japan wrote with China in 1905 a long supplementary agreement—using this method because she instinctively follows tortuous ways, believing that this gives her an opportunity to defend herself against accusations of expropriation—and against actions which would be beneath the dignity of the Imperial House, but which her commercial appetite forces her to take.

In the supplementary treaty, Japan solemnly declared (Article II) that " in view of the earnest desire expressed by the Imperial Chinese Government to have the Japanese and Russian troops and railway guards in Manchuria withdrawn as soon as possible, and in order to meet this desire, the Imperial Japanese Government, in the event of Russia agreeing to the withdrawal of her railway guards, or in case other proper measures are agreed to between China and Russia, consent to take similar steps accordingly." What has been the result of this undertaking ? Japan has made secret agreement after secret agreement with Tsarist Russia—

the last one in 1916, a few months before the Russian Revolution—to secure at all costs that Russia should take no such action, her recent intrigues with General Horvath, the Tsarist agent who was left in control of the Chinese Eastern Railway, being dictated with the same aim and object, namely, to prevent at all costs her "sister-nation," China, being repossessed of her sovereign rights. During the past two years, when every trace of Russian soldiers has been removed from Northern Manchuria, Japan, so far from being willing to execute Article II, has increased her garrison. In the remaining articles of the supplementary treaty Japan annexes everything of value she can think of in Southern Manchuria, her policy being *ruthless commercial and industrial exploitation*, where Russia was content merely to dominate. Friction between China and Japan has been ceaseless in Manchuria ever since, the smaller country never hesitating to use threats and pressure on the slightest provocation. The latest illustration of this is the forced introduction of Japanese paper currency by the hundred million yen and the attempt to make it the standard.

It was probably because of the difficulty which she experienced in annexing Korea that Japan determined in 1915 to settle the results of her belligerency with Germany in a new way. In the matter of Korea, in spite of her successful war against Russia, she had been forced to enter into four successive conventions with the Seoul Government before the deed was completed; and during all this time the press and peoples of the Far East were in a state of uproar. There was first an agreement on 17th November, 1905, which placed the control and direction of the foreign relations in her hands; another on 31st July, 1907, by which all administrative measures and all high official appointments were made subject to the approval of a Japanese Resident-General; still another on 12th July, 1909, whereby the administration of justice and prisons—the essential police-power—was given her; and a final one on 23rd August, 1910, when Korea was publicly annexed to the Japanese Empire and the Emperor of Korea deprived of his rightful title. Consequently, by filing the famous Twenty-one Demands on China, almost immediately after Tsingtao had been captured, when every indication from the European war-theatre pointed to a drawn war, and forcing through, by means of an ultimatum, all those clauses which did not directly conflict with the treaty rights of other Powers, Japan imagined she was safe, and would be able to do from her Shantung base—Kiaochow—all she had done in Manchuria acting from the Port Arthur territory.

The nature of the things Japan thinks she has won by means of this manœuvre can easily be described; and it should be carefully noted that in these matters, as in all other essential political business, the German standard has been the one scrupulously followed. Japan has placed the Manchurian railways and the Port Arthur lease on ninety-nine-year Kiaochow terms—an action which is absolutely *ultra vires*; and, moreover, she has not only taken over all the German enterprises in Shantung *by force*, but she has pushed through, by means of loans to the now destroyed pro-Japanese party, a railway extension scheme on a German-made plan, secretly prepared by Germany before the European war, aiming at making Tsingtao the sea-terminus for a railway system which at some distant date is to stretch through Central Asia and link up with the Middle East.

The problem growing out of Manchuria and Shantung has therefore a new character. It is no longer a local Far Eastern problem: it is a world-problem which has to be faced and solved, or else there will be fresh world-disaster.

IV

One final aspect has to be made clear.

Until the death of Yuan Shih-kai, Japan treated China as a country with a united government which could be held responsible and which must be treated with; after his death she deliberately abandoned this policy and dealt with specified persons as fully authorized agents whom she seduced to her point of view, and used as her instruments. No longer using the Chinese Foreign Office as her channel of communication, she boldly commenced making secret agreements with individuals, and by means of her agents in the Ministries of Communications and Finance she was able under cover of the World War to do untold harm. Adopting the simple principle that the " postponed " Group V of the Twenty-one Demands was her principal business with the Republic, she has for years sought to do piecemeal and secretly what she failed to do openly, i.e. to get into her hands, or into the hands of her agents, control of Chinese arms and munitions; control of strategic areas, control of important railways

IF JAPAN REFUSES? 117

and control of industrial monopolies. How many secret agreements in all she has made no one accurately knows, but the number actually listed is remarkable enough.[1] In defiance of the precise terms of the Anglo-Japanese Alliance Treaty, which calls upon her to communicate fully and frankly with her ally, Japan's watchword in Peking and throughout the provinces has been obscurantism and nothing but obscurantism, with disastrous results for the future well-being of the Chinese people.

And here it is necessary specially to note that until Viscount Ishii made his historic pilgrimage to Washington in 1917, and induced the United States to write the indiscreet Lansing-Ishii Notes, she was forced to hold her horses; no sooner were the Notes in her archives than she began to act in an imperious way. China had created a so-called War Participation Bureau, i.e. a Special Military Office, with a number of well-equipped divisions depending upon it, nominally for dealing with the question of organizing an expeditionary force to proceed to France, but in reality (since it was under the control of the Northern military party) to continue the fight with the South and crush Canton. For a number of months this amiable object was assiduously pursued, fed by funds from Japan acquired by secret agreements, and with not the slightest regard for China's international pledges. Although France went so far as to offer to finance a Chinese expeditionary force, division by division as they were shipped, and drew up many memoranda to that end, Japan

---
[1] The reader is referred to the remarkable list of loans and mortgages in Appendix C.

saw to it that the plan was killed. When intervention in Siberia seemed inevitable in May 1918, Japan signed with the War Participation Bureau the secret Sino-Japanese military agreement in a last effort to defeat America's plan of helping Russia. By creating a new international imbroglio in which railways, Bolsheviks, and Tsarists of the stamp of General Horvath would be so mixed as to defy a solution, she added to the chaos beyond Lake Baikal; and since the armistice of the 11th November she has managed for three years to keep garrisons on one excuse or another in every strategic point on the Siberian seaboard.

The root of the evil lies in the present nature of the Japanese Government; in the fact that under the present Constitution it is perfectly legitimate for the Japanese Ministry of War to direct the Empire's policy in China and Siberia and to be above the control of the Diet. A Japanese Cabinet, directly responsible to the Diet under the Constitution, is absolutely essential to the peace and happiness of the Far East; unless that, as well as a proper extension of the franchise, can be acquired by constitutional means, so that the Japanese people can act as a check on their own bureaucracy, it is essential to oppose Japanese intimidation of China by methods other than those adopted during the war.

For it is force that is behind the Japanese programme—not equity or justice, but force, mixed with corruption. This force is to-day semi-antiquated, for Japanese armaments, no matter how much they have been expanded, are totally unequal to the challenge offered to first-class maritime

Powers with great interests to protect in the Far East. Indeed, it is obvious to observers on the spot that the asset of geographical isolation has been exhausted, and that Japanese policy has acquired the dangerous quality of a gamble with fate.

Japan stands at the cross-roads. It is for her to elect what her future is to be: whether the bacillus of imperialism is to be blown out by explosion, or dissipated by reform. Korea cries aloud for decent treatment—Korea can to-day rightfully demand either Home Rule or proper representation of her people in Japan's Diet. Here, if there ever was a case, is a country which should be administered only under a mandate derived from a League of Nations; for what has Korea done that she should be treated as a conquered province? and why should Manchuria and the province containing the birthplace of Confucius—Shantung—be menaced by the same fate? It is not true that these regions are necessary for the overspill of the Japanese population, for they are densely populated and are not attracting Japanese immigrants. Korea, which has been under the Japanese heel for seventeen years, has to-day less than 500,000 Japanese immigrants, or a net increase of 400,000 persons since the Russo-Japanese War. During this period the Korean population has increased by over 3,000,000, and in less than two decades the land will be far more crowded than Japan. In the case of Manchuria, experience has not only conclusively proved that the Japanese cannot compete as farmers with the Chinese—that is, they cannot go on the land—but in petty trade the Chinese are ousting them, the

Japanese being able to retain their hold only by a system of preferential treatment and anti-Chinese regulation which they assiduously enact in the Port Arthur leased territory and along the zone of the South Manchuria railway in a last effort to justify their claims, their so-called gold currency measures being the latest device. As for Shantung, that has long been so densely populated by the native race that vast numbers of men must go annually to other provinces—particularly to Manchuria—to find food, the villages in Shantung being so thick on the ground as to form continuous chains. It is not sufficiently known that since 1900 the population of China has increased by 68 millions—that is, by considerably more than either the present population of Germany or Japan; and that by the middle of the present century the Chinese cannot number less than 500 millions. Although Japan's northernmost island of Hokkaido is practically uninhabited and could carry 12 million people at the lowest computation, she vainly tries to push her people on to the Asiatic mainland so as to justify her so-called Asiatic Monroe Doctrine, which means for her not the protection but the subjection of the East. Hating to go abroad save to the white man's lands, where they earn great profits rapidly and easily, the Japanese care so little for their annexed territories that the Japanese population of Formosa has long been stationary, if it has not actually receded. Town-dwellers by instinct, leaving much of their agriculture to women, who labour early and late in the fields, for them foreign parts have no attractions. Colonization is indeed alien to their natures; it is their military leaders who are trying almost by force to make them build a fabric of empire in the extraordinary manner we have indicated.

There is no more to be said—not a word. We have placed the problem under the searchlight; we have indicated the solution. The Imperial Conference recently assembled in London has shown by the negative results reached in the matter of the Anglo-Japanese Alliance that the British Empire is divided and has no definite policy in Eastern Asia. The London Cabinet, whilst proclaiming that the loyalty Japan showed during the War demanded the renewal of the Anglo-Japanese pact, was faced with the certainty that such renewal would split certain of the Dominions from the Mother Country. Being furthermore unwilling to reveal publicly that this "loyalty" during the War did not hesitate to demand a free hand in Borneo and the Dutch East Indies in 1916 as the price for military co-operation in Mesopotamia and the Near East at the lowest ebb of British war-fortunes, they were driven after six weeks' vain debate to adjourning the discussion to the Washington Conference under the transparent device that there had been no effective Treaty denunciation. Remembering what has been recorded in these pages concerning the fatal muddle made in August 1914 regarding China's entry into the War, it must be said that no greater failure of British diplomacy has been recorded than this handling of an inherently simple question. Still the problem must be solved. If there is justice enough left over after Europe has settled her own troubles, Eastern Asia is surely the first claimant. But unless that precious quality is used in abundance, the day is not far distant when the crash will come and men must fight again. The group which behind the scenes controls the Republic in Peking, as in Canton, is determined that that shall come if there is no other honourable solution, and ways and means now exist which have hitherto been entirely lacking.

APPENDICES

APPENDIX A

THE ANGLO-JAPANESE ALLIANCE TREATY

Signed JULY 13, 1911

PREAMBLE.

THE Government of Japan and the Government of Great Britain having in view the important changes which have taken place in the situation since the conclusion of the Anglo-Japanese Agreement of August 12, 1905, and believing that the revision of that Agreement responding to such changes would contribute to general stability and repose, have agreed upon the following stipulations to replace the Agreement above mentioned, such stipulations having the same object as the said Agreement, namely :—

A. The consolidation and maintenance of the general peace in the regions of Eastern Asia and India.

B. The preservation of the common interests of all the Powers in China by insuring the independence and integrity of the Chinese Empire and the principle of equal opportunities for the commerce and industry of all nations in China.

C. The maintenance of the territorial rights of the High Contracting Parties in the regions of Eastern Asia and of India and the defence of their special interest in those regions:—

Article 1.—It is agreed that whenever, in the opinion of either Japan or Great Britain, any of the rights and interests referred to in the preamble of this Agreement are in jeopardy, the two Governments will communicate with one another fully and frankly, and will consider in common the measures which should be taken to safeguard those menaced rights and interests.

Article 2.—If by reason of an unprovoked attack or aggressive action, wherever arising, on the part of any other Power or Powers, either of the High Contracting Parties shall be involved in War in defense of its territorial rights or special interests mentioned in the preamble of this Agreement, the other High Contracting Party will at once come to the assistance of its Ally and will conduct the war in common and make peace in mutual agreement with it.

Article 3.—The High Contracting Parties agree that neither of them will, without consulting the other, enter into a separate agreement with another Power to the prejudice of the objects described in the preamble of this Agreement.

Article 4.—Should either of the High Contracting Parties conclude a Treaty of general arbitration with a third Power, it is agreed that nothing in this Agreement shall impose on such contracting party an obligation to go to war with the Power with whom such an arbitration treaty is in force.

Article 5.—The conditions under which armed assistance shall be afforded by either Power to the other in circumstances entered into the present Agreement, and the means by which such assistance is to be made available, will be arranged by the military and naval authorities of the High Contracting Parties, who will from time to time consult one another fully and frankly upon all questions of mutual interests.

Article 6.—The present Agreement shall come into effect immediately after the date of its signature, and remain in force for ten years from that date.

In case neither of the High Contracting Parties should have notified twelve months before the expiration of the said ten years the intention of terminating it, it shall remain binding until the expiration of one year from the day on which either of the High Contracting Parties shall have denounced it. But if, when the date fixed for its expiration arrives, either Ally is actually engaged in war, the Alliance shall, *ipso facto*, continue until peace is concluded.

APPENDIX B

TEXT OF THE LANSING-ISHII NOTES

DEPARTMENT OF STATE, WASHINGTON,

November 2, 1917.

EXCELLENCY,
     I have the honour to communicate herein my understanding of the agreement reached by us in our recent conversations touching the questions of mutual interest to our Governments relating to the Republic of China.

In order to silence mischievous reports that have from time to time been circulated, it is believed by us that a public announcement once more of the desires and intentions shared by our two Governments with regard to China is advisable.

The Governments of the United States and Japan recognize that territorial propinquity creates special relations between countries, and, consequently, the Government of the United States recognizes that Japan has special interests in China, particularly in the parts to which her possessions are contiguous.

The territorial sovereignty of China, nevertheless, remains unimpaired, and the Government of the United States has every confidence in the repeated assurances of the Imperial Japanese Government that, while geographical position gives Japan such special interests, they have no desire to discriminate against the trade of other nations or to disregard the commercial rights heretofore granted by China in treaties with other Powers.

The Governments of the United States and Japan deny that they have any purpose to infringe in any way the independence or territorial integrity of China, and they declare, furthermore, that they always adhere to the principle of the so-called " open door," or equal opportunity for commerce and industry in China.

Moreover, they mutually declare that they are opposed to the acquisition by any government of any special right or privileges that would affect the independence or territorial integrity of China, or that would deny to the subjects or citizens of any country the full enjoyment of equal opportunity in the commerce and industry of China.

I shall be glad to have your Excellency confirm this understanding of the agreement reached by us.

Accept, Excellency, the renewed assurance of my highest consideration.

ROBERT LANSING.

His Excellency,
  VISCOUNT KIKUJIRO ISHII,
    Ambassador Extraordinary and
    Plenipotentiary of Japan, on
    Special Mission.

APPENDIX C

JAPANESE SECRET LOANS TO CHINA IN 1918

	Yen.
1. Mitsui Bussan Kaisha to the Central Government on the Bureau of Engraving and Printing	2,000,000
2. Yokohama Specie Bank's share of Group Bank advance for flood relief	200,000
3. Mitsui Bussan Kaisha to Military Governor of Chihli for military purposes	1,000,000
4. Second advance on Second Reorganization Loan by the Yokohama Specie Bank	10,000,000
5. Japanese Syndicate to rebel government of the Province of Hunan	20,000,000
6. Yokohama Specie Bank to the Central Government for suppression of plague	1,000,000
7. Loan to the Province of Fukien for general purposes	1,000,000
8. Mitsui Bussan Kaisha to Chihli Province for purchase of yarn for spinners for flood relief	1,000,000
9. Tai-hei Kumei Syndicate to Central Government for purchase of arms	14,000,000
10. Second loan to Bank of Communication made by Bank of Chosen, Bank of Taiwan and Industrial Bank	20,000,000
11. Chosen Group of Banks to Telegraph Administration for extension of lines	20,000,000
12. Loan to Fengtien Province made by the Bank of Chosen	3,000,000
13. Loan to Shihpingkai–Chengchiatun Railway made by Specie Bank	2,600,000
14. Nanjin Railway Loan—between Nanchang and Kiukiang	100,000

15 Wireless Loan	3,000,000
16 Loan to Chihli Province by the Chosen Bank	1,000,000
17. Kirin-Huaining Railway Loan by Banks of Chosen, Taiwan, and Industrial Bank of Japan	20,000,000
18. Loan to Shensi Province	2,000,000
19. Yokohama Specie Bank of Hupeh Province	1,000,000
20. Okura Forestry Loan made by Industrial Bank of Japan and the chosen group of Banks	30,000,000
21. Kirin Forestry Loan made by Industrial Bank of Japan and the Chosen Group Banks..	30,000,000
22. Second Reorganization Loan—third advance	10,000,000
23. Loan on Yu Kan Iron Mines, Kiangsi Province	3,000,000
24. Loan to Shantung Province	1,500,000
25. Peking Telephone Loan	5,000,000
26. Manchurian and Mongolian Railway Loan	40,000,000
27. Shantung Railway Loan	26,000,000
28. Military Agreement Loan	20,000,000
29. Peking-Suiyuan Loan	4,000,000

These twenty-nine loans amounted to Yen 246,400,000, or, say, £30,000,000. The Chinese Government of the day, composed of Ministers now in hiding in the Japanese Legation in Peking, used the most valuable national assets, such as mines, railways and industrial organizations, as security for them. The conferring of orders and decorations by the Japanese Government upon nine officials " in recognition of the services rendered with regard to loans to China " is one of many proofs to substantiate this statement. Among those nine officials are Mr. Shoda, late Finance Minister; Mr. Ichiki, late Vice-Minister of Finance; Mr. Shinno, Director of the Financial Bureau in the Finance Department; Dr. Kobayashi, Japanese Financial Agent at Peking; Mr. Shoda and Mr. Ichiki being recipients of the First Order of the Sacred Treasure. Mr. Nishihara, who was active in 1918 in securing loans for Japan, was not decorated, perhaps because he is not an official. The Japanese Government has also con-

APPENDIX C

ferred a number of orders and gold cups upon military officers " in recognition of the service rendered in connection with the conclusion of the Sino-Japanese Military Agreement." Japan's object in encouraging reckless borrowing by the Chinese Government was undoubtedly to secure control of China's finances.

APPENDIX D

THE SHANTUNG RAILWAY AGREEMENT OF SEPTEMBER 24, 1918

Communications between the Japanese Foreign Office and the Chinese Minister to Japan.

The Shantung Railway Agreement of September 24, 1918, was signed by the Chinese Minister to Japan, but was not ratified by the Chinese Government. Japan advanced $10,000,000 on the strength of the agreement, and the Japanese Minister to Peking now states that there is no reason why the agreement should have been ratified by China, as it is binding upon her in any case. The question is asked : " Can the Minister of any Power make with the State to which he is accredited a treaty that is binding, without further ratification, upon his own government ? " If so, a new and very far-reaching principle in international law will have been established.

It will be observed that under this secret agreement Japan proposes to garrison permanently the capital of Shantung Province, to control the police along the railway zone, and to place the Shantung railway under " joint control." These steps are tantamount to annexation.

TEXT OF AGREEMENT.

Minister of Foreign Affairs, Tokio,
    to
H. E. Chang Tsung Hsiang,
    Chinese Minister to Tokio.

FOREIGN OFFICE, TOKIO,
September 24, 1918.

SIR,
    In view of the neighbourly feelings of friendship between our two countries, the Government of Japan, being

APPENDIX D 133

desirous of arranging matters in a spirit of harmony, has drawn up an agreement which it regards as a satisfactory settlement of all outstanding questions relating to the Province of Shantung, and I now have the honour to bring this proposal to the notice of your Government. The terms of the proposed agreement are as follows :—

I

All Japanese troops stationed along the Shantung Railway —with the exception of one regiment which will be left at Tsinan—will be withdrawn to Tsingtao.

II

The Chinese Government may establish a Police Force which shall take over the duty of guarding the railway.

III

The Administration of the Shantung Railway shall set aside a sufficient sum to meet the expenses of the Police Force.

IV

Japanese subjects are to be employed at the Headquarters of this Police and at all important stations and in the Police Training School.

V

Among the employees of the Shantung Railway posts shall be given to Chinese subjects also.

VI

After it has been definitely decided to whom the Shantung Railway is to belong, the railway is to be placed under the joint management of China and Japan.

VII

The Civil Administration Offices now in existence are to be abolished.

I have the honour to request that you will communicate to me views of your Government with regard to the above proposal.

I have, etc.,
(*Signed*) BARON GOTO,
Japanese Minister for
Foreign Affairs.

CHINESE MINISTER'S REPLY.

Chang Tsung Hsiang,
Chinese Minister at Tokio,
to
Japanese Minister for Foreign Affairs.

TOKIO
(*No date*).

SIR,
I have the honour to acknowledge receipt of your letter couched in the following terms :—

(Quotes in full letter from Minister for Foreign Affairs of September 24, 1918.)

I have the honour to inform you that the Government of China accepts with pleasure the proposal contained in the letter quoted above.

I have, etc.
(Seal of CHANG TSUNG HSIANG,
Envoy Extraordinary and
Minister Plenipotentiary.)

APPENDIX E

KIRIN AND HEILUNGCHIANG MINING AND FORESTRY AGREEMENT

NOTE.—This agreement is a good illustration of Japanese secret methods : for a sum equivalent to three million pounds sterling the forests and mines of the two northernmost Manchurian provinces, with an area hardly inferior to France and Germany, and worth incalculable sums, are mortgaged in such a way as to give Japan prior rights. This agreement must be broken.

For the object of developing the Mining and Forestry industry in Kirin and Heilungchiang Provinces, the Government of the Republic of China (hereafter called the First Party) agrees to conclude a loan for thirty million yen (Yen 30,000,000) with the Tsung Hua Hwai Yi Bank (hereafter called the Second Party). The Articles which are agreed to by the two Contracting Parties are as follows :—

1. The total amount of this loan is thirty million yen.
2. The term of the loan is ten years, which therefore expires on the 1st of August, 1928. But the loan may be continued by a further arrangement between the said Parties at the expiration of the above stipulated term.
3. Five years from the date of signing this Agreement, however, a part of the loan may be repaid after a prior notice of six months.
4. The interest on this loan is $7\frac{1}{2}$ per cent. annually, which is Y7.50 for every 100 yen, but for any additional term as provided for in Article 2 the rate of interest shall be fixed again according to the state of the money market.
5. The payment of the first instalment of the interest, which begins from the date of the paying over of the

loan up to the 14th of January, 1919, shall be made in advance by the First Party. After that, every six months' interest shall be paid in advance on the 15th of January and 15th of July of every year. But the last interest payment shall be made by a calculation carried up to the last day of the term of loan and be paid in advance.

6. The payment of this loan will be made fully without any deduction.
7. The payment of the principal and interest shall be made in Tokio, Japan.
8. The security of this loan is as follows:—
   (a) The Mines and Governmental Forests in the Kirin and Heilungchiang Provinces.
   (b) The Governmental income on the production of the above mentioned Mines and Forests.
9. If the First Party wishes to conclude any other loan with other Parties, using the above mentioned Mines and Forests or the Governmental incomes as security, an arrangement must be first made with the Second Party.
10. This Agreement shall be void when full redemption of capital and interest have been made.

This Agreement is in Japanese and Chinese, three copies in each language. The Ministry of Agriculture and Commerce, the Ministry of Finance, and the Second Party shall each retain one copy of both Japanese and Chinese. If there is dispute regarding the meaning, the Japanese copy shall be considered authoritative.

      TIEN WEN LIH, Minister of the Ministry of Agriculture and Commerce.
      TSAO RU LIN, Minister of the Ministry of Finance.
      LU TSUNG YU, the General Manager of the Tsung Hua Hwai Yi Bank.
      SHIH-NAN-CHAUNG-TSE-LONG, the Japanese Business Manager of the Tsung Hua Hwai Yi Bank.

August 2, 1918.

APPENDIX F

ARTICLES FROM THE JAPANESE CONSTITUTION DEFINING THE AUTOCRACY OF THE JAPANESE GOVERNMENT

NOTE.—The following Articles from the Constitution of Japan give some idea of the autocratic and unrepresentative character of the Japanese Government and disclose the manner in which power is concentrated in the hands of a military and civil bureaucracy without parliamentary checks.

This is particularly illustrated by Article 71—even the control of the purse being placed beyond the scope of the Diet, which is made powerless in the matter of supplies by the provision that Budgets can be automatically re-enacted from year to year.

The " reforms " introduced in 1919 by the present Hara government do not touch these things : the franchise-qualification has merely been lowered from 10 yen in direct taxes to 3 yen, which will increase the electorate from 1,460,000 to 2,860,000 voters, and still leave great classes of educated men without the vote. Ordinary manhood suffrage, on the basis of the present population, would give Japan at least 13 million voters. Ten million men are therefore left without the vote. The increase of the number of constituencies from 381 to 464 is a step in the right direction ; but the Koreans are entirely without representation, nor has Formosa any voice at all—the 3 million Formosans being treated like the 17 million Koreans as a conquered race.

Article 3.—The Emperor is sacred and inviolable.

Article 4.—The Emperor is the head of the Empire, combining in Himself the rights of sovereignty, and exercising them according to the provisions of the present Constitution.

Article 5.—The Emperor exercises the legislative power with the consent of the Imperial Diet.

Article 12.—The Emperor determines the organization and peace standing of the Army and Navy.

Article 13.—The Emperor declares war, makes peace, and concludes treaties.

Article 55.—The respective Ministers of State shall give their advice to the Emperor, and be responsible for it.

Article 67.—Those already fixed expenditures based by the Constitution upon the powers appertaining to the Emperor, and such expenditures as may have arisen by the effect of law, or that appertain to the legal obligations of the Government, shall be neither rejected nor reduced by the Imperial Diet, without the concurrence of the Government.

Article 68.—In order to meet special requirements, the Government may ask the consent of the Imperial Diet to a certain amount of Continuing Expenditure Fund for a previously fixed number of years.

Article 71 —When the Imperial Diet has not voted on the Budget, or when the Budget has not been brought into actual existence, the Government shall carry out the Budget of the preceding year.

APPENDIX G

THE MANCHURIAN AND MONGOLIAN (SECRET) RAILWAY AGREEMENT

EXPLANATORY NOTE.—This document, secretly signed in Tokio on the 28th of September, 1918, by the Chinese Minister to Japan, acting under instructions not of the Chinese Government but of the Ministry of Communications, is of the utmost importance for the Japanese plan of the envelopment of Peking and North China by a railway network.

The reader is invited to study the matter on the map. Then it will be seen that the New Manchurian-Mongolian Railway project, if allowed to pass unchallenged, will not only monopolize these areas to Japanese influence, but will allow Japan to get control of a new seaport just beyond the Great Wall at Shanhaikwan.

There is little doubt, although the agreement purposely leaves the name a blank, that Hu-lu-tao, an ice-free harbour which was to have been the terminus of the Anglo-American Chincho-Aigun Railway, is meant. This harbour has been developed by British engineers and nearly a million sterling spent on it. It is a magnificent natural harbour superior to Dairen, and it is plain that Japan covets it.

Although the preliminary agreement that follows calls for the signature of a final agreement within four months from the 26th of September, 1918 (i.e. before the 28th of January, 1919), nothing further has been done in the matter owing to the immense outcry which this matter has raised in China.

The Government of the Republic of China (hereinafter called the Government) for the purpose of constructing railways from Jehol to Taonan, from Changchun to Taonan, from Kirin to Kaiyuan through Hai-lung, and from a point on the Jehol-Taonan Railway to a seaport (hereinafter called the Four Railways of Manchuria and Mongolia), agrees to conclude a contract with a syndicate representative of the Industrial Bank of Japan, the Bank of Taiwan, and the Bank of Chosen (hereinafter called the Banks) in the terms of the following Preliminary Agreement in anticipation of the Formal Agreement :—

1.—The Government recognizes and approves of the project to construct railways from Jehol to Taonan, from Changchun to Taonan, from Kirin to Kaiyuan, and from a point of Jehol-Taonan Railway to a seaport ; and the Banks will issue Gold Bonds for the Government of the Republic of China, which will be called the Gold Bonds of the Jehol-Taonan Railway, the Gold Bonds of the Changchun-Taonan Railway, the Gold Bonds of the Kirin-Kaiyuan Railway, and the Gold Bonds of the extension railway (hereinafter called the Gold Bonds of the Four Railways of Manchuria and Mongolia).

The railway line from a given point on the Jehol-Taonan Railway to a given seaport will be mutually arranged between the Government and Banks.

2.—The Government shall make a statement of the necessary expenditure for the construction of these four railways and obtain the consent of the Banks for the same.

3.—The term of the Gold Bonds of the Four Railways of Manchuria and Mongolia shall be forty years, and the repayment of the principal in annual instalments shall commence from the eleventh year from the date of issue.

4.—As soon as the Government concludes the Formal Agreement regarding the said Four Railways of Manchuria and Mongolia with the Banks, the plan for the construction work shall be arranged between both the Parties without further delay.

5.—The following will be the security of the issuing of

APPENDIX G 141

the Gold Bonds of the Four Railways of Manchuria and Mongolia :—

The properties and income of the Four Railways of Manchuria and Mongolia now and in the future.

The Government may not offer the above-mentioned properties or the income derived therefrom as the security to any other Party without the approval of the Banks.

6.—The price and rate of interest of the Gold Bonds of the Four Railways of Manchuria and Mongolia will be arranged between the two Parties at the time of issue.

7.—The Articles concerning the above which have not been provided for shall be mutually arranged between the Government and the Banks.

8.—This Preliminary Agreement will be the basis of the formal agreement of the Four Railways of Manchuria and Mongolia which shall be made within four months from the date of signing this preliminary agreement.

9.—An advance of 20 million yen in full amount without commission will be made by the Banks at the time of the signature of the preliminary agreement.

10.—The interest on such advance will be at the rate of 8 per cent. annually, which is 8 yen annually for every 100 yen.

11.—On the paying over of this advance, National Treasury Notes will be issued in exchange for the cash.

12.—The said National Treasury Notes will be renewed once every six months, and on each renewal the interest of the prior six months will be paid over to the Banks.

13.—When the formal agreement of the Four Railways of Manchuria and Mongolia is signed, the money received from the issue of the said Gold Bonds shall be employed in part for the repayment of these advances.

14.—The paying over of the advances as well as the payment of interest, with all other details, shall be carried out in Tokio, Japan.

142 THE TRUTH ABOUT CHINA AND JAPAN

This Preliminary Agreement is in Chinese and Japanese, two copies being made of each. The Government and the Banks shall each retain one copy in Chinese and Japanese. If there is any dispute, the Japanese text will be considered the authoritative one.

This Preliminary Agreement is signed on the 28th of September, 1918.

      CHANG TSUNG HSIANG,
        The Chinese Minister to Japan.
      SIAO YA IN-ERH LONG,
        The Vice-President of the
          Industrial Bank of Japan.

APPENDIX H

THE SHANTUNG RAILWAY EXTENSION AGREEMENT

EXPLANATORY NOTE.—The railway agreement annexed completes the network of contracts rapidly entered into by the militarist elements in Tokio and Peking prior to the German collapse and the armistice of November 11th.

It will be observed that this Shantung Railway Extension Agreement, like the Four Manchurian and Mongolian Railway Agreement and the unratified Kiaochow Railway Agreement (Document D), was rushed through at the end of September, 1918, to complete the pernicious militarist programme drawn up by Japan and her Chinese tools before the fall of the Terauchi Cabinet in Tokio and the Tuan Chi Jui Cabinet in Peking.

Its importance is not so great as the Manchurian-Mongolian Agreement, everything depending on the future status of the German Shantung Railway (Chinanfu to Tsingtao). If this railway is completely restored to China, the fact that Japan has building contracts west and south of the Shantung provincial capital will not be very important. If the Shantung Railway is not completely restored to China, these projected extensions will hasten the Manchurianization of the central China territory.

The following is a translation of the Chinese text of the Tsi-Shun and Kao-Hsu Railways published by the *Wai-chiaopu* :—

PREAMBLE.

For the construction of the railways from Tsinan (Shantung) to Shunteh (Chihli) and from Kaomi (Shantung) to Hsuchow (Kiangsu) (hereinafter called the Two

144 THE TRUTH ABOUT CHINA AND JAPAN

Railways), the Government of the Chinese Republic (hereinafter called the Government) enters upon the following Agreement, a protocol to the final Loan Agreement with the Representative of the Japanese Industrial Bank (hereinafter called the Bank) which represents the Japanese Industrial Bank, the Taiwan Bank and the Bank of Korea :—

Article 1.—In order to meet the expenditure for the construction of the Tsinan-Shunteh and Kaomi-Hsuchow Railways, the Government will entrust the Bank for the issue of the Chinese Government Tsi-Shun Railway Gold Loan and the Chinese Government Kao-Hsu Railway Gold Loan (hereinafter called the two Railway Loans).

If it is found after due investigation that the lines fixed will not be profitable for business, the Government may negotiate with the Bank for alterations and changes.

Article 2.—The Government shall at once draw up an estimate for the various expenses in connection with the two railways and submit same to the Bank for approval.

Article 3.—The term of the loan shall be forty years; and in the eleventh year of its issue, the redemption shall commence by instalment in each year.

Article 4.—As soon as the Formal Loan Agreement is signed between the Government and the Bank, the construction shall begin.

Article 5.—The Government shall give the following security to the Bank for the payment of coupons and the redemption of the loan :—

All the properties and the incomes of these two railways, both the present and the future.

Without the permission of the Bank the Government shall not make use of the above properties and incomes as security to a third party.

Article 6.—As to the price of the bonds, the rate of interest and the net proceeds to be received for the two railway loans, they shall be fixed in accordance with the circumstances of the time and the interest of the Government.

APPENDIX H 145

Article 7.—All details which have not been provided for in this Agreement shall be fixed between the Government and the Bank.

Article 8.—This Agreement shall form the basis for the Formal Loan Agreement of these two railways, which shall be signed four months after its conclusion.

Article 9.—After the signing of this, the Bank shall make an advance of Japanese 20,000,000 yen to the Government without conmmission or any deduction.

Article 10.—The interest of the above advance shall be 8 per cent., i.e. 8 yen per year for each 100 yen.

Article 11.—A similar amount of the Government Treasury Bonds shall be given by the Government for the above advance.

Article 12.—In a period of each six months these bonds shall be changed, when an interest for this period shall be given to the Bank.

Article 13.—After the conclusion of the Formal Loan Agreement the Government shall refund the above advances by the proceeds first realized by the sale of the bonds.

Article 14.—The transactions connected with the delivery of the proceeds, the payment of interest and the redemption of the above advance shall be done in Tokio.

Two copies of the above agreement shall be made in Chinese and Japanese, and one each be kept by the Government and the Bank. Should doubts arise in any point, the Japanese version shall be followed.

(*Signed*) CHANG CHUNG-HSIANG
and " HSIAO-YA-YIN ER LAN."

Dated 29th day, 9th month of the 7th
Year of the Chinese Republic, etc.

In addition to the above there are two notes addressed to the Japanese Foreign Minister by Mr. Chang Chung-hsiang, stating that the Chinese Government has decided to contract loans from the Japanese capitalists for the construction of the following railways :—

1.—Between Kaiyuan, Hailung and Kirin.
2.—Between Chanchung and Taonan.
3.—Between Taonan and Jehol.
4.—A second line between Taonan and Jehol.
5.—Between Tsinan and Shunteh.
6.—Between Kaomi and Hsuchow, etc.

The Japanese Foreign Minister's Note states that in order to cement the good relations between the two Neighbouring Nations, the Japanese Government has made the following proposals in connection with the Shantung Problem :—

1.—With the exception of Tsinan, all the Japanese troops along the Kiaochow-Tsinan Railway shall be withdrawn to Tsingtao.
2.—The police forces for the protection of the Kiaochow-Tsinan line shall be organized by the Chinese Government.
3.—An adequate amount of money shall be paid by the Kiaochow-Tsingtao Railway to meet the expenses of the above police forces.
4.—Japanese shall be engaged in the police headquarters, training institutes, etc.
5.—Some Chinese shall be selected and appointed officers for the Kiaochow-Tsinan Railway.
6.—It is now definitely fixed that the Kiaochow-Tsinan Railway and its offices shall later on be under the joint control of the Japanese and the Chinese.
7.—The civil offices which have now been established shall be abolished.

All the above communications were duly acknowledged and approved by either party.

APPENDIX I

TEXT OF SINO-JAPANESE WIRELESS INSTALLATION AGREEMENT

EXPLANATORY NOTE.—The annexed Wireless Telegraph Agreement is important to complete the general survey of the methods which Japan has used and is still using to get control of China.

By virtue of this agreement Japanese agents for a period of thirty years will control the central wireless installation of the capital of China—that is, if they can build the station, which is extremely doubtful. In the matter of wireless, as in all scientific work, the Japanese are mere copyists, their wireless work being extremely imperfect.

It should be noted that the British Marconi Company had a preliminary agreement for this installation on a purely commercial basis, but that lack of proper diplomatic support, coupled with Japanese intrigue and money, allowed this Japanese invasion to take place.

It is proposed to erect in China a great Wireless Telegraphic Installation that shall be capable of communicating telegraphically direct with Japanese, European or American great installations. The conditions of agreement are as follows :—

1. This Agreement is contracted by the Chinese Ministry of the Navy of the one part (hereinafter called " the Chinese Government ") and by Messrs. The Mitsui Co., a Japanese firm, undertaking the contract (hereinafter called " the Contractors ") of the other part, and the two contracting parties have mutually agreed upon the conditions of this Agreement.

2. The Chinese Government have consented to allow the Contractors to erect a great wireless installation whose forwarding and receiving apparatus shall be capable of communicating messages with Japan, Europe and America. The site of the installation shall, after being designated by the Chinese Government, be either bought or leased for the purposes of erection.

3. The cost for the lease or purchase of lands, erection of buildings and masts or towers, and the construction, transport and erection of the plant, etc., is estimated to be £536,267 (the estimates are attached hereinafter), a sum which the Contractors shall raise and shall also assume entire responsibility for all matters connected with the construction and equipment.

4. The above mentioned capital sum of £536,267, which is for the purpose of constructing the telegraphic installation, shall be repaid in thirty equal annual instalments, that is to say, the whole of this capital shall be divided into thirty equal parts, of which one part shall be paid each year. The part that remains unpaid shall bear interest at the rate of 8 per cent. per annum, to be included in the yearly instalment of repayment. The date for each yearly instalment of repayment shall be fixed to be on the 31st of December, Solar Calendar, to commence from the year that operations begin.

5. The Contractor's security for the above capital and for the annual interest shall be from the remaining balance of the receipts of the telegraphic installation after due deduction of all disbursements that are to be drawn from that source, hence the Contractors have to assume sole responsibility for the repayment of all disbursements; should the receipts be insufficient to meet the disbursements, then for the repayments of capital and interest the Contractors shall also assume responsibility, but the Chinese Government shall confer upon the Contractors full controlling powers within the period of thirty years' duration.

6. During the period of sole control of the telegraphic installation by the Contractors, the Chinese Government shall be entitled to a royalty of 10 per cent. of the receipts of the workings of the telegraphic installation, which is to be calculated in accordance with the whole year of the Solar

APPENDIX I 149

Calendar and shall be payable at the end of each year. Should the receipts earned for the whole year's working of the telegraphic installation be insufficient to cover the payments of disbursements, then the Chinese Government shall still be entitled to a 10 per centum of the total receipts collected during the whole year.

7. The Chinese Government have power to appoint officers in the installation to oversee and supervise accounts, in order that a proper check may be established over the royalty as set forth in Article 6. Besides the appointment of above-mentioned officials, students may be appointed to practise at the station, but the Chinese Government shall bear the whole of the expenses that these students may cost.

8. Owing to the very great responsibility involved with regard to receipts of the working of the station, the Chinese Government must accord its assent to unrestricted communication with wireless stations in all foreign countries and with seaports and ships, with a view to future development, but in communication with wireless stations in the interior of China, with the exception of military communications which shall obey the orders of military organizations, all other commercial communications in the interior of China shall be uniformly refused acceptance. In the event of the Chinese Government being on a war footing this station shall obey all martial orders laid down in China.

9. At any time within the thirty-year period, the Government may take back for itself the station. At that time all outstanding balance yet unpaid and accrued interest of 8 per cent. up to that date shall be wholly liquidated by the Chinese Government; the Contractors shall then at the same time have vitiated all their rights of movements *vis-à-vis* the station. According to the above-mentioned procedure, the Contractors shall previous to the handing over of the station to the Chinese Government make an inventory in the Chinese and English languages of all articles and things that compose the station and present the inventory to the Ministry.

150 THE TRUTH ABOUT CHINA AND JAPAN

Government must Recognize Contractors' Proprietary Rights in Case of Failure of Payment.

10. Should the Chinese Government be unable to repay the sums in accordance with what is stipulated in Article 9, then the Government has no power to remove from the Contractors their control of the station. Should the Government act in any manner of such a nature it must recognize the Contractors' possession of proprietary rights over the Telegraphic Station.

11. Since the Contractors have to bear the responsibility of repayment of capital and payment of annual interest during the term of thirty years, therefore the Contractors have the right to transfer the Telegraphic Station to another company, but the consent of the Chinese Government must be obtained, otherwise it would not be lawful.

12. At the end of the period of thirty years (should provision of Article 9 have not been acted upon), then, irrespective of the capital having been totally redeemed or otherwise, this Telegraphic Station shall then wholly be handed over to the Chinese Government without price, and the Government shall take over the Station, the Contractors making demand for no recompense whatsoever, but the Government shall give six months' previous notice, otherwise the Contractors shall appropriate a 5 per cent. of the annual receipts up to the fifth year as remuneration.

Personnel of Station must be Retained after Redemption of Loan.

13. After the Chinese Government shall have taken over the Telegraphic Station as a Government property, the service of the personnel of the Station shall be retained by the Government, who shall pay them their cash salaries. Should there be anyone unsuitable, that person may be discharged from the service, but during the term of control by the Contractors all members of the staff shall be found by the Contractors, who shall pay them their salaries, such salaries shall be drawn from the receipts of the Station.

14. Should greater power be added or additional plant

APPENDIX I 151

be purchased during the term of thirty years of control of the Station by the Contractors, the Contractors shall assume responsibility for such augmentations, but the consent of the Chinese Government for such addition of capital outlay must be obtained, and the repayment of such additional outlay shall still be within the same period of thirty years as aforesaid—that is, devoted to repayments of capital and payment of interest.

15. The Chinese Government shall issue *huchows* (exemption certificates) for the Contractors to facilitate the transport of all kinds of machinery material, and exempt such from *likin* and other inland miscellaneous charges, but the Contractors must furnish full lists of all machinery material in order that they may be examined, and then *huchows* be issued for these consignments. As to other matters, the regular ordinary regulations in force in China shall be followed.

16. Should Chinese products of suitable quality and cheaper price be available for use among the material needed for the Telegraphic Station, such products shall be given first preference.

17. This Agreement is done in three exemplars, each in the Chinese and English languages. Should there arise any difference in interpretation of any point, the English version shall be the authoritative text.

(*Signed*) The Ministry of the Navy of the Republic of China.
The Representative of Messrs. The Mitsui Co.

Done in the
7th Year of the Republic of China,
on the 21st Day of February.

NOTE TO THE MINISTRY OF THE NAVY FROM MR. OMURA, REPRESENTATIVE OF MESSRS. MITSUI & CO.

February 21*st.*

GENTLEMEN,
With reference to the Supplementary Articles of Agreement, in Article 2 it is stated that while the control of the Telegraphic Station is assumed by the Chinese Govern-

ment all disbursements and the service of the amortization of the capital and interest payments shall be wholly assumed by the Chinese Government, should your Ministry entertain misunderstandings as to this Clause, our firm is willing to undertake the control of the Station on behalf of your Government under instructions from your Government, and our firm will also undertake to repay capital and interest and all disbursements shall be paid, and act in accordance with the Articles of conditions as agreed upon in the Proper Agreement. The three clauses set forth below are for the purpose of safeguarding the interests of our firm and are as follows :—

1. The Chinese Government must give one year's previous notice in order that reliable measures as to procedure may be devised.

2. During the period that the Telegraphic Station is under the control of the Chinese Government, the interest on the capital and all disbursements shall be borne by the Chinese Government independently in accordance with the stipulations set forth in the present Agreement.

3. During the period that the Telegraphic Station is under the control of our firm, our firm shall be allowed to collect charges for transmission of all official and commercial messages.

With respects, etc.

This note is attached to the end of the Supplementary Articles Agreement. As both parties are mutually agreeable, this is sealed in testimony.

Ministry of the Navy of the Republic
of China.
Representative of Messrs. Mitsui Co.

SUPPLEMENTARY ARTICLES TO THE AGREEMENT.

The Ministry of the Navy (hereinafter called " the Chinese Government ") with the Japanese firm, Messrs. Mitsui & Co., the contracting engineers (hereinafter called " the contractors "), have mutually come to an agreement upon

APPENDIX I

supplementary articles, in the 7th year, on the 21st day of February, for the construction of a wireless telegraph station.

According to the agreement the Chinese Government may at any time repay the outstanding unpaid balance and take over the station as a Government property.

Now it is agreed that the procedure to be adopted after the completion of the erection of the telegraph station is that the station shall be immediately taken over by the Chinese Government. The expenses necessary for its erection shall be raised by the contractors for the Chinese Government, hence the following supplementary articles have been mutually agreed upon by the Chinese Government and the contractors, and are as follows :—

1. The contractors undertake to raise a loan for a total sum of £536,267 for the Chinese Government, which shall be placed to the credit of the contractors in a Japanese bank for the purpose of constructing a wireless telegraph station.

2. The repayment of the above-mentioned capital sum by the Chinese Government shall be spread over thirty years, that is to say, the total capital shall be divided into thirty equal parts, and one part shall be repaid each year, amounting to a sum of £17,875 11s. 4d. ; the unpaid outstanding balance shall bear interest of 8 per cent. per annum, to be payable on the same date as the date of repayment of the annual instalment, to which it shall be added.

3. The date of repayment of capital each year shall be fixed to be on December 31st of the Solar Calendar. The first year for commencing the repayment shall be from the tenth year after the year that the station commences to operate after its construction and erection are completed and it can communicate telegraphically with the stations erected in Japan, Europe and America.

4. The rate for the repayment of interest by the Chinese Government shall be according to Article 2 of the Supplementary Agreement, and interest shall commence to be paid on December 31st of the year that the erection of the telegraph station is completed.

5. According to this agreement of supplementary articles, since the control of the telegraphic station and the powers

154   THE TRUTH ABOUT CHINA AND JAPAN

of its commercial management shall be taken over again by the Chinese Government, therefore, should the telegraphic station receipts from its workings be deficient to meet the payment of disbursements and so forth, the contractors shall not assume any responsibility, and Article 5 of the proper agreement shall also be vitiated.

6. After the taking over again of the telegraphic station by the Chinese Government should in the course of its commercial operation there arise any impediment from other overseas cable companies with whom the Chinese Government have already entered into any agreements, then the contractors shall act under the instructions of the Chinese Government, whereby the contractors shall devise means to remove any restrictive conditions by negotiation with those cable companies with the station, and should no satisfactory solution be arrived at, then the repayments of the instalments that the Chinese Government ought to repay shall be postponed for the time being until some solution shall have been come to, after which repayments may be resumed.

7. The present supplementary article of agreement shall be an integral part of the proper agreement, and shall be identically acted upon in accordance with Article 17 of the proper agreement.

(Ministry of the Navy of the Republic of China) (The Japanese firm, Mitsui & Co.; Representative, Omura). Done in the 7th year of the Republic of China, on the 21st day of February.

NOTE TO THE MINISTRY OF THE NAVY, FROM MR. OMURA.

GENTLEMEN,
        The agreements entered into between your Government and the Great Northern and Eastern Extension Cable Companies state that prior to the year 1930 no other land telegraph station shall be allowed to communicate telegraphically with Europe and America and so forth: our firm shall duly respect this clause within the year limit prior to the year 1930, as provided for in Article 8 of our Supplementary Articles Agreement. From the year 1931 your

APPENDIX I 155

Government's agreement with the Great Northern and Eastern Extension Cable Companies will terminate and lose its virtue, and our firm then shall be able to connect with Europe and America and all the world round by commercial communication without restriction. We therefore hereby make this declaration, and respectfully request you to take note. This note is attached to the end of our Supplementary Articles Agreement. As both parties are in mutual agreement, seals are affixed in testimony. (Mitsui & Co.), February 21st.

TO THE MINISTRY OF THE NAVY, FROM MR. OMURA.

GENTLEMEN,
 The agreement that our firm has entered into with your Ministry for the construction of a great wireless telegraph station, all the necessary material required is selected from noted factories in Japan, and is either purchased from Europe or America, and is of the best quality, and in no case will any inferior material be employed in substitution. We hereby make this declaration and respectfully request you to take note. This note is attached to the Supplementary Articles Agreement, and as both parties are in agreement, seals are affixed in testimony (Mitsui & Co.; Representative, Omura), February 21st.

DECLARATION.

Whereas the Proper and Supplementary Agreements for the construction of a large wireless telegraph station were completed on February 21, 1918, and whereas it is mutually agreed by both parties that during the term of thirty years no other party shall be allowed to erect a similar wireless telegraph station for communicating telegraphically with Japan, Europe and America, neither may the Chinese Government itself erect an installation, and the Cabinet have in meeting passed the application; and whereas the conditions of the agreement have been mutually agreed upon and the agreement has been signed by both the contracting parties at the end of the document, and, furthermore, the statement as set forth in the preceding has been mutually agreed upon by both the contracting parties and that the procedure set forth in Article 17 of the Proper Agreement shall be adopted.

7th year of the Republic of China, March 5th. (Mitsui & Co., Omura.)

For Product Safety Concerns and Information please contact our EU representative GPSR@taylorandfrancis.com
Taylor & Francis Verlag GmbH, Kaufingerstraße 24, 80331 München, Germany

www.ingramcontent.com/pod-product-compliance
Lightning Source LLC
Chambersburg PA
CBHW070621300426
44113CB00010B/1609